WHITE REFLECTIONS ON BLACK POWER

WHITE REFLECTIONS ON BLACK POWER

CHARLES E. FAGER

WILLIAM B. EERDMANS PUBLISHING COMPANY
GRAND RAPIDS, MICHIGAN

Permission to quote from copyrighted materials is hereby acknowledged with gratitude.

Amsterdam News, quotations from following issues: July 16, 1966 (Stokely Carmichael), Aug. 27, 1966 (James Jackson), Sept. 10, 1966 and Oct. 15, 1966 (C. Philip Randolph), Oct. 29, 1966 (George L. P. Weaver), and Nov. 5, 1966. All reprinted by permission.

Elsie Archer, *Let's Face It*. Copyright © 1959 by Elsie Archer. Published by J. B. Lippincott Company, and reprinted with permission from the publisher.

James Baldwin and Budd Schulberg, "Dialog in Black and White," *Playboy*, Dec. 1966. Copyright © 1966 by HMH Publishing Co., Inc.

John Benson, "Interview with Stokely Carmichael," *The Militant*, May 23, 1966. Reprinted by permission.

Francis L. Broderick and August Meier, editors, *Negro Protest Thought in the Twentieth Century*. Copyright © 1965 by The Bobbs-Merrill Company, Inc. Reprinted by permission of the publishers.

Stokely Carmichael. "What We Want." *The New York Review of Books*, Sept. 22, 1966. Copyright © 1966, by Student Nonviolent Coordinating Committee. "Toward Black Liberation," *The Massachusetts Review*, Autumn 1966. Copyright © 1966 by Student Nonviolent Coordinating Committee.

Kenneth B. Clark, *Dark Ghetto*. Copyright © 1965 by Kenneth B. Clark. Reprinted by permission of Harper & Row, Publishers.

Samuel Du Bois Cook, "The Tragic Myth of Black Power," *New South*, Summer 1966. Reprinted with permission of the Southern Regional Council, Inc., *New South*, Summer, 1966. Copyrighted.

David Danzig, "The Meaning of Negro Strategy," *Commentary*, Feb. 1964. Quoted from *Commentary*, by permission; copyright © 1964 by the American Jewish Committee.

James Farmer, *Freedom When*. Copyright © 1965, by Random House, Inc.

John Fischer, "Letter to a New Leftist from a Tired Liberal," *Harper's Magazine*, Mar. 1966. Copyright © 1966 by Harper's Magazine, Inc. Reprinted from the Mar. 1966 issue of *Harper's Magazine* by permission of the author.

Paul Jacobs and Saul Landau, editors, *The New Radicals*. Copyright © 1966, by Random House, Inc.

Malcolm X, *Autobiography*. Copyright © 1964 by Alex Haley and Malcolm X.

Gene Marine, "I've Got Nothing Against the Colored, Understand," *Ramparts*, Nov. 1966. Copyright © 1966 by Ramparts Magazine, Inc.

Meet the Press, America's Press Conference of the Air, the National Broadcasting Co., produced by Lawrence E. Spivak, Sunday, Aug. 21, 1966. Reprinted by permission.

Hans Morgenthau, "Truth and Power," *The New Republic*, Nov. 1966. Reprinted by permission of *The New Republic*, copyright © 1966, Harrison-Blaine of New Jersey, Inc.

The New York Times: "Excerpts from the Vice President's Speech to NAACP Convention," July 7, 1966; C. E. Vanderwarker, Jr.'s, letter to Editor, July 23, 1966; "Excerpts from Paper on Which the 'Black Power' Philosophy Is Based," Aug. 5, 1966; Editorial on "The Politics of Frustration," Aug. 7, 1966; Rev. George Kalbfleisch's letter to Editor, Aug. 19, 1966; *New York Times Book Review*, Sept. 11, 1966: Richard Bone, "A Black Man's Quarrel with the Christian God." Copyright © 1966 by The New York Times Company. Reprinted by permission.

Carl Rowan, "Crisis in Civil Rights Leadership," *Ebony*, Nov. 1966. Copyright © 1966 by Johnson Publishing Co., Inc.

Bayard Rustin, "Black Power and Coalition Politics," *Commentary*, Sept. 1966. Quoted from *Commentary*, by permission; copyright © 1966 by the American Jewish Committee.

Barry Sheppard, "Interview with CORE Leader," *The Militant*, Aug. 8, 1966. Reprinted by permission.

Charles E. Silberman, *Crisis in Black and White*. Copyright © 1964 by Random House, Inc.

James A. Wechsler, "Labor in Retreat: The AFL-CIO Tragedy," *The Progressive*, Jan. 1966; and "Killers of the Dream," *The Progressive*, Dec. 1966. Reprinted from *The Progressive* magazine, Madison, Wisconsin.

Roy Wilkins, in *The Crisis*, Aug.-Sept. 1966. Reprinted by permission.

Whitney Young, "Wide Open Split Among Negro Leaders," *The National Observer*, Oct. 10, 1966. Reprinted by permission.

Whitney Young, *To Be Equal*. Copyright © 1964 by Whitney M. Young, Jr.

Dedication

To my wife, Tish,
first of all

To Mr. Randolph T. Blackwell,
*whose investment of time, money, and confidence in me
may herein begin to show returns;*

To James and Diane Bevel,
*instructors and companions through a
trying and glorious period;*

To Dr. Arthur H. Cash,
*professor and advisor:
if there is any virtue in this piece,
it reflects your discipline and example.*

APOLOGY TO THE READER

This essay is not really about Black Power or the Negro movement. It is, rather, an extended meditation on what demands for action spring from a serious personal commitment to making American society a just and fit place for authentic human existence. The exploration undertaken in the following pages, therefore, is not presented as a detached survey and critique of our culture.

My background is Northern, urban, middle-class, college-educated, secular-oriented, New Left and *white;* all of these factors (above all, I think, color) condition the questions asked and the directions the inquiry takes. Likewise, the answers, the imperatives sought, are those specific to a Northern, urban, middle-class, college-educated, secular-oriented, "New Left" white person's condition, needs, and aspirations. If the results of this investigation have any more than personal significance, I would expect them to be useful mainly to other whites of similar background who are also seeking a direction, a "strategy" for their lives, which can be both personally meaningful and effective in contributing to real, humanizing change in our social institutions.

Such a search for direction seems to me the underlying impulse behind almost all New Left thought and action. Thus far, however, the New Left has not, it seems to me, produced a direction or strategy that can satisfy its search. I am hopeful that the directions that suggested themselves to me in the course of these reflections — none of which are

7

really original — can be of some value to the reader, as they have been to me.

The meditations I have described take place quite appropriately, even necessarily, in the context of an attempt to come to grips with the meaning of Black Power. Contact with the Negro struggle was, more than any other, *the* event in my life (and, I think, in the lives of many like me). This struggle made it inevitable that some of us would break through the accepting silence of the fifties in which we were raised and demand to know what our world, our society, our lives were *really* all about. The Negro struggle was the best vantage point from which we could begin to see some of the realities we were after; so we gravitated to it naturally, and it taught us much. But before Black Power, most of what the movement taught us was about *others* — Southern whites, the "Power Structure," the Administration, the police, the welfare system, etc. It did not tell us (or at least we successfully avoided hearing) about *ourselves*. So while it shattered some of our illusions about society, it enabled us to preserve and foster other illusions about ourselves. These illusions, I now think, were bound sooner or later to collide with the development of the blacks' struggle.

With the emergence of Black Power this collision came — head on. Because of it, we whites have been forced to look at ourselves and our role in producing meaningful social change without the crutch the civil rights movement provided. Such a re-examination is — it has been for me — a painful process, as, I suspect, is most real growth.

The course of this process is set down in the following pages. I have done my level best to be accurate in my account of Black Power and fair in stating positions with which I disagree. But what errors there are remain my responsibility.

It seems to me that, after some recent events in our Republic, it is only prudent for me to assure my readers that this essay was conceived, researched, written and revised without any help whatsoever (to the best of my knowledge, belief and intention) from the staff or funds of the Central Intelligence Agency. I would like to acknowledge and express appreciation for the help I did receive from the thinking of Herbert Appleton Wagner III, from the living example of Lawrence C. Carter, Jr., and from the sure fingers of Carol Browne, Laurel Cornell, and Roger Polk, all of whom are my associates at Friends World Institute.

— C.E.F.

Friends World Institute
Westbury, New York
March, 1967

CONTENTS

APOLOGY TO THE READER   7

CHAPTER ONE:
    THE ELEMENTS OF BLACK POWER   13

CHAPTER TWO:
    THE IDEOLOGY OF THE LIBERAL COALITION   52

CHAPTER THREE:
    LIBERALS AND BLACK POWER   83

CHAPTER FOUR:
    THE LIBERAL TASKS   97

CONCLUSION   106

NOTES   109

BIBLIOGRAPHY   115

Chapter One

THE ELEMENTS OF BLACK POWER

"There are," writes Bayard Rustin, "two Americas — black and white — and nothing has more clearly revealed the divisions between them than the debate currently raging around the slogan of 'black power'."[1] It is difficult for most whites to grasp the profundity of the gaps between their experience and the Negroes' experience. The divisions between the two Americas are obscured by the language and social institutions that the races have superficially in common, as well as by patterns of life that discourage all but myth-reinforcing interracial contacts. But the divisions are real and deep, and they spring in large measure from the fact that while both races live in the same social, political, cultural and economic *milieu,* their experiences in this *milieu* have been opposite and contradictory. Let us look briefly at a few of these divisions.

Perhaps the most basic division is the historical one. Most whites came to America voluntarily, from a situation thought to be bad to a situation viewed as at least potentially better. And for most of them, or their children, life here was indeed quantitatively, if not always qualitatively, more abundant. White groups who came here hoping to preserve a religion or cultural identity were by and large able to do so, though not without struggle. But the Negro came here a slave, ripped brutally out of his African motherland and borne across the Atlantic in chains. His awareness of his own history, his culture, his family life, his religion, even

13

his original name — all were virtually blotted out, and barriers were erected against their rediscovery that are only now being overcome. For two hundred years he remained the white man's property. Even after the Emancipation most blacks were not far from *de facto* slavery. And tragically for the nation, the same institutions that made possible the prosperity of the incoming whites were involved, both as beneficiaries and partisans, in the enslavement and exploitation of blacks. This cruel paradox, paid for by the continual dilution of our national idealism with, in Lincoln's term, "the base alloy of hypocrisy," has continued to the present, and has been consistently reflected in the attitudes of both races. Most whites can see some of its effects on the Negro. But few whites even suspect that it has marked *us* just as surely. This historical division between the prosperous freeman and his world view on the one hand, and the oppressed slave and his world view on the other, is the foundation of the wall between the "two Americas."

Consider what this division has meant in terms of a particular institution, the law. The law in America has the stated function of protecting citizens and their property. But in the master-slave relationship the law could hardly function the same for the white citizen and property owner as it did for his black piece of property. Men could and did do to their property what they could not do to other citizens. It was illegal to let a slave read books[2]; it was necessary, because of what white male citizens did to their black female property, to declare all slave offspring illegitimate.[3] Reconstruction brought temporary changes in the effects of the law for Negroes, but it did so only because the dominant Republicans found this politically advantageous. When this situation no longer appeared advantageous, the ex-slaves were left to the devices of their former masters. Today, both in the South and in the North, the law appears to Negroes as the force that keeps them in "their place." The law subjects them to the whims of its enforcers, while it is unable to make good on its own written pledges of equality in employment, education, housing, or simple protection.

New York City is a good example of how the law works for Negroes. A municipal law outlawing discrimination in housing financed wholly with private funds (the first law of its kind in the nation) has been in force since 1958; but here is a summary of the law's achievements:

> New York has both a State Commission on Human Rights and a parallel City Commission. The procedures for securing redress, however, ordinarily require knowledge and patience on the part of the plaintiff which cannot in fairness be expected of someone merely looking for a decent place to live. Moreover, although one apartment may be "opened" after tortuous procedures, there is no deterrence to further violations, no carryover effect. Each negotiated enforcement of the law remains an isolated event, and so members of a minority have little confidence in the efficacy of registering complaints. Recently, New York's two agencies proudly announced a "great increase" in complaints received, but the *total* amounted to a mere 528 complaints in the first half of 1966. Philadelphia's counterpart agency, the Commission on Human Relations, has received only 466 complaints in the entire three years since a fair-housing ordinance was adopted.[4]

Enforcement of equal job opportunity, now a part of federal statutes, presents an even bleaker picture. In eighteen months of operation, the federal Equal Employment Opportunity Commission has amassed a backlog of over 80,000 cases, and has for months been short two of its five members.[5]

What can a phrase like "respect for law and order," a favorite among "conservative" and "liberal" whites alike, mean to a people for whom "law and order" have always amounted to tools for maintaining an oppressive status quo?

Consider, for another example, the schools. Education has with much justification been seen by most minority groups in American history as the major avenue to social and economic mobility. But for the Negro, despite individual successes, this simply has not been true. The color bar does not drop automatically for the black man with a white sheepskin. Kenneth Clark cites data indicating

> that Negroes who have completed four years of college "can expect to earn only as much in a lifetime as whites who have

not gone beyond the eighth grade." This is true both in the North and in the South. The white high school graduate will earn just about as much as a Negro who has gone through college and beyond for graduate training.[6]

The government, private philanthropy, churches, and even some civil rights groups unite in urging Negro youths to stay in or go back to school. Yet the unemployment rate for Negro young people is better than one third anyway. The realization of the not-much-brighter future which awaits even educated blacks gives the lie to all the "stay in school" slogans. And the young people know it:

> When a warlord of one of the last of Harlem's active fighting gangs was asked why he did not go downtown and get a job, he laughed and replied:
> "Oh come on. Get off that crap. I make $40 or $50 a day selling marijuana. You want me to go down to the garment district and push one of those trucks around and at the end of the week take home $40 or $50 if I'm lucky? They don't have animals doing what you want me to do. There would be some society to protect animals doing what you want me to do. I'm better than an animal, but nobody protects me. Go away, mister, I got to look out for myself."[7]

In the absence of real training for meaningful social and economic mobility, the function of the schools for Negroes has become largely custodial, a way of keeping large numbers of excess children off the streets. Naturally, this fact is not lost on the students. How can whites expect black youths to react with anything other than indifference or scorn to injunctions about staying in such institutions, no matter how sincerely the advice is offered?

These are but suggestions, hints of the magnitude and variety of obstacles standing in the way of even elementary understanding between the two Americas. Examples could be multiplied, but as Bayard Rustin said, ". . . nothing has more clearly revealed the divisions between them than the debate currently raging around the slogan of 'black power'." We shall examine first the elements of Black Power and then the debate, as a case study in the lack of communication between the two Americas.

It is not as difficult to understand Black Power as it has been made out to be. Since the slogan was first used, Stokely Carmichael, former Chairman of the Student Nonviolent Coordinating Committee and the most widely known exponent of the "new" concept, has himself appeared frequently on television, has been interviewed repeatedly in the press, and has written at least two major articles dealing with the definition and ramifications of Black Power (see Bibliography). The ideas behind the concept have remained consistent and clear as he has presented them to both white and Negro audiences. Thus the controversy regarding the meaning of the phrase must be regarded as largely self-generated. It is either the reaction of observers and interpreters whose preconceptions about the Negro movement make it hard for them to understand the concept, or the result of deliberate obfuscation and sensationalism. Later we will examine in detail the major criticisms of Black Power.

A Second Look at Integration

The first term which must be redefined if whites are to understand Black Power is "integration." Integration has at least two meanings in discussion today, both of which the Black Power spokesmen have rejected: (1) integration as tokenism, and (2) integration as assimilationism. Let's look closer at these kinds of integration. Stokely Carmichael has spoken bitterly of the first type of integration:

> I'll take an example from Lowndes County (Alabama). Last year five Negroes entered the white school. All the papers hailed this as a great triumph. Finally Lowndes County had been cracked. But all the other Negro children had to go to the same old schools. And no whites went to the black schools, because they were in fact inferior.[8]

Lowndes County is nearly 80 percent Negro, and the attendance of five black children in white schools cannot be regarded as having much, if any, meaningful impact on the lives of that 80 percent. Lowndes County is not exceptional, nor can its degree of "integration" be regarded as the beginning of significant change to come. Bayard Rustin, surveying the pace of school integration *nationwide,* tells us:

> If in 1954 when the Supreme Court handed down the desegregation decision, you had been the Negro parent of a first-grade child, the chances are that this past June you would have attended that child's graduation from a segregated high school.[9]

Token integration consists of installing a black face or two in a white-controlled institution, creating an interracial facade but affecting neither the white control of the institution nor the exclusion of the mass of blacks from it. Most of the "integration" which has come about since 1954 has been of this kind, whether in schools, employment, housing, or politics. Many of us white liberals decry it, but we have yet to do much about it.

Integration in its other commonly accepted sense implies the assimilation of Negroes into a larger and presumably "colorblind" society. This has long been the goal of most liberal whites and many civil rights organizations. James Farmer, the former National Director of the Congress of Racial Equality, has written almost nostalgically about that organization's dedication to this kind of integration:

> No organization was so aggressively colorblind, so ideologically committed to the utter irrelevance of race, as we. If only the races could get to know each other — living, working, playing in each other's sight — what purpose would there be to note a man's race? Our work and fellowship in CORE during those early years were dominated by these sentiments: members of both races strove to make sure that color wouldn't count in our daily activities, even as it wouldn't count in the Great Day that was coming. One of CORE's first pamphlets was called "Erasing the Color Line"; sometime later it was revised and retitled "Cracking the Color Line."[10]

It is difficult to find an explicit statement of integration as assimilationism. But a good picture of the concept and its meaning is given by Whitney Young, Executive Director of the National Urban League, in his book, *To Be Equal:*

> We are, through integration, seeking to help all our citizens realize their true, creative potential and to move toward

a new type of society that is not a replica of any past culture or any single group, but is a culture that has absorbed the best from each.

Today only hopelessly insecure, tragically immature people need to surround themselves with sameness. People today who are secure and mature, people who are sophisticated, want diversity. One doesn't grow, one cannot be creative, one cannot develop by living and associating with, going to school and church only with people who look like oneself, have the same backgrounds, the same religion, the same interests.

... Instead of conforming to exclusiveness, people ought to conform to inclusiveness. I hope that we will be able to create the kind of society wherein people will have to apologize for sameness — for an all-white school or neighborhood or church — because this would be an indication of their immaturity, their lack of sophistication and security. We want a society where people will boast of diversity and the fact that their churches, their businesses, their schools and their neighborhoods are like little United Nations. This will be an indication that they are mature and secure human beings.

My concept of integration is not one of either the white or the Negro giving up all that he is used to. After honest examination of the positive and negative elements in each of the two cultures, we will retain the best in each.... It is not a matter of Negroes giving up all that has been part of their community, their background and their culture and adopting all that is white. Out of the years of suffering and deprivation the Negro has developed certain qualities — humaneness, compassion, patience and endurance — and certain values that should be useful to whites either as individuals or in organizations such as General Motors or the Bank of America.

It was these qualities of perseverance, patience, resilience, of ability to adjust and adapt that were the sustaining pillars of Negro life.... These qualities are important to this nation which finds itself in a situation of leadership that is severely challenged, one in which it must make compromises and must adapt.[11]

The elements of assimilationism are here: the objective is a "little United Nations" in all our institutions, where racial diversity will be quite frankly a status symbol; this will come about through a process of absorbing the "best" qualities from each group into an as-yet-unrealized "new type of society." Since Negroes are only 10 percent of the population, such a new society would require them to be distributed pretty evenly within the larger institutions, if everyone were to be able to "boast of diversity," and be sophisticated, mature, and secure. The Negro in this "new type of society" would retain his "positive" qualities and shed his "negative" ones. It is worth noting that most of the "positive" qualities Young specifies — patience, endurance, "ability to adjust and adapt" — are of the kind he believes are likely to be regarded as useful in employees of such status quo institutions as General Motors or Bank of America. We are left to presume that these corporations are among the "positive" elements of white society to be retained in the new order. Who can, reading these words, fail to hear the echoes of Booker T. Washington's Atlanta Exposition Address: "To those of the white race ... were I permitted I would [say], 'Cast down your bucket among those people who have, without strikes and labor wars, tilled your fields, cleared your forests, builded your railroads and cities, and brought forth treasures from the bowels of the earth. . . .' " Young says nothing of the Negro's cultural heritage beyond his mention of the potential "usefulness" of some "qualities" it has produced; the implication is that in the new society there will not be any distinct black sub-group.

An example of how this philosophy is likely to work out in practical recommendations for Negroes can be found in the pages of a small book, *Let's Face It,* by Mrs. Elsie Archer. The book is a "guide to good grooming for Negro girls," and is recommended by both the NAACP and the National Urban League. The assumptions the book makes about color are revealed in an offhand remark in the first chapter: "You know, already, that the color of your skin is not important. There isn't anything you can do about it anyway, and you want to know how to make it make you the beauty you want to be."[12] After discussing health, cleanliness, and figure control in a manner typical of such writing — and without ever mentioning race — the basic point of view comes to the surface in somewhat more detail when the author reaches the

physical characteristic which, next to skin color, is most un-
deniably "Negroid," i.e., tightly curled hair:

> Up to this chapter [the author declares], your personal
> problems are not too different from those of any other girl
> your age. You are built exactly like any other girl, in fact
> you might even be prettier and smarter than some; your skin
> may so easily be the same color as hers but you think there
> is a difference and that the difference shows. When we
> come to the discussion of hair, you feel pretty sure that this
> is where the difference begins. Hold on there! This is not
> exactly true.
>
> There is a large percentage of girls with skin either
> the same color as yours, or a little darker or lighter that
> are not faced with a difference in the grade of their hair,
> at all. But if you're on the other side of the fence, there is
> a difference and you're anxious to do something about it.
> Sure, it has made you wonder many times... Why did I
> have to have this kind of hair? You're not alone with such
> thoughts and the color of your skin doesn't enter into it.
> Girls of other races worry and complain about their hair, too.
> Many of these girls have hair that is so tightly curled that
> they, too, must resort to hair straightening methods. In fact,
> some months ago, one of our national fashion magazines ad-
> vertised an electric comb that will shape (a nice way to say
> "pull out") and soften hair that is too curly and unmanage-
> able. In areas where beauty shops cater to other races, there
> are many that advertise "hair straightening." The burden may
> become easier when you know you don't carry it alone.
>
> Instead of wishing for the "fairy godmother" to come
> down and touch you with her magic wand that will give you
> a new head of hair, you can put your time to better use....
> If Mother Nature wasn't as good to you as she should have
> been, it's up to you to give her a helping hand.[13]

Mrs. Archer, it seems to me, makes two assumptions in
her writing: *first,* that differences between the races are almost negligible and certainly of no importance, and *second,*
that such visible differences as there may be, especially tightly
curled hair, are at bottom undesirable and are best dealt with
by minimizing or concealing their divergence from the norm.
Mrs. Archer is not pessimistic about this approach; in fact,
she is quite confident about it, especially where hair is concerned: "Things have never been so good for pressed (straight-

ened) hair. The progress of pressed hair is on the up and up. No hair problem is so great that it can't either be corrected or greatly improved."[14] It would not seem rash to me if we were to draw from these remarks a suspicion that in Whitney Young's "new type of society," Negroid hair is one of the less "positive" characteristics which will not be retained. Nor does it seem unfair to suggest that a similar fate would await other "Negroid" traits — cultural as well as physical — which could not pass the litmus test of "usefulness" to such as General Motors or Bank of America.

This is perhaps the assimilationist's major flaw: that in his "new type of society," the Negro's place and contributions always wind up being judged by the white status quo. What is good about Negroes in this new age will be — to paraphrase Young and a former General Motors head — whatever is good about Negroes for GM and Bank of America.

Stokely Carmichael has characterized this form of integration with sardonic accuracy:

> Its goal was to make the white community accessible to "qualified" Negroes; and presumably each year a few more Negroes, armed with their passports — a couple of university degrees — would escape into middle-class America and adopt the attitudes and life-styles of that group, and one day the Harlems and Watts will stand empty, a tribute to the success of integration.[15]

It may also be clear now why Negroes, as James Farmer writes, seemed to know something about this new "colorblind" society that whites did not:

> ...We learned that America couldn't simply *be* colorblind. It would have to *become* colorblind and it would only *become* colorblind when *we gave up* our color. The white man, who presumably has no color, would have to give up only his prejudices. We would have to give up our identities. Thus, we would usher in the Great Day with an act of complete self-denial and self-abasement. We would achieve equality by conceding racism's charge: that our skins were an affliction; that our history is one long humiliation; that we are empty of distinctive traditions and any legitimate source of pride.[16]

We begin to see now the underlying dynamics of integration by assimilation: it takes for granted that all the characteristics of middle-class, white (mainly white Anglo-Saxon Protestant), American society are the primary objects of aspiration. Each year some unknown thousands of light-skinned Negroes "pass" as white, moving into white neighborhoods, and living undetected as Negroes in a white world. Integration by assimilation proposes in effect to permit *all* blacks thus to "pass" and become indistinguishable — except for their particularly "useful" (to whites) characteristics.

One of the realities this approach ignores is the fact that the attitudes and life-styles of middle-class white Americans are highly specific, relative characteristics which have been shaped by many historical and cultural factors; and they are by no means universal, even among middle-class whites. This kind of integration suggests a new version of the famous American "Melting Pot." But as Charles Silberman points out in *Crisis in Black and White:*

> ... The crucial thing about the melting pot was that it did not happen: American politics and American social life are still dominated by the existence of sharply defined ethnic groups. To be sure, these groups have been transformed by several generations of life in America. . . . And yet the ethnic groups are not just a political anachronism; they are a reality. The WASPS (White Anglo-Saxon Protestants), the Irish-Americans, the · Italian-Americans, the Jewish-Americans do differ from each other in essential ways. They vote differently, raise their children differently, have different ideas about sex, education, religion, death, etc. And so if Negroes are to assimilate, if they are to integrate with the white American, the question has to be asked: with *which* white American? With the WASP? Or with the Irishman? The Italian? The Slovak? The Jew?[17]

The ethnic pluralism of white America isn't likely to dissolve into a homogeneous new culture, at least not in the foreseeable future. Thus the assimilationist's dream, if it is a serious one, turns into a task of proportions far greater than we had been led to expect. Nor is it entirely certain that this pluralism is wholly undesirable, that it automatically suggests immaturity, insecurity, or a lack of sophistication among the members of the ethnic groups. Each immigrant group has had to grapple with the problem of preserving while reconciling its ethnic heritage with the patterns and demands of life in their new home. For most, the process is still going on; but it has rarely, if ever, meant the complete abandonment of the heritage. Negroes, like the rest of us "immigrants" (though of course they preceded most of us), presumably will have to forge, as did other groups, some new synthesis between their culture and their homeland, a job made infinitely more difficult for them by white America's systematic obliteration of their roots. Silberman concludes his discussion of the meaning of cultural pluralism thus: "What history suggests is that when the Negro solves his problem of identity, he will have gone a long way towards finding the means of relating himself to every other American group."[18]

Assimilationism almost totally ignores this need for self-discovery by implying that all the identity black people need is whatever they have that is useful to whites, or to white-dominated institutions. Why, then, should we be surprised to hear Stokely Carmichael characterize it thus:

> This concept of integration had to be based on the assumption that there was nothing of value in the black community, and that little of value could be created among blacks. So the thing to be done was to siphon off the acceptable Negroes into the surrounding middle-class white community.[19]

It might be thought that this is overstating the case. Yet it seems unlikely that Negroes who for so long have been forced to understand and manipulate the real attitudes and prejudices of whites simply in order to *survive*, would misunderstand the actual meaning of assimilationism.

We have seen that Negroes who have "arrived," or who expect to arrive, take assimilation quite literally to the extent of bleaching their skin, straightening their hair, and even undergoing surgery to thin "Negroid" nostrils. Most whites have no conception of the lengths to which some Negroes go and the pain they inflict upon themselves in order to imitate white characteristics. Malcolm X wrote in his *Autobiography* of attempts at imitation:

> I'd guess that eight out of ten of the Hill Negroes of Roxbury (Boston), despite the impressive-sounding titles they affected, actually worked as menials and servants. "He's in banking," or "He's in securities." It sounded as though they were discussing a Rockefeller or a Mellon — and not some gray-headed, dignity-posturing bank janitor, or bond house messenger. "I'm with an old family" was the euphemism used to dignify the professions of white folks' cooks and maids who talked so affectedly among their own kind in Roxbury that you couldn't understand them. I don't know how many forty- and fifty-year-old errand boys went down the hill dressed like ambassadors in black suits and white collars, to downtown jobs "in government," "in finance," or "in law." It has never ceased to amaze me how so many Negroes, then and now, could stand the indignity of that kind of self-delusion.[20]

Nor was Malcolm, in his youth, free from trying to be white. Here is his not untypical account of the first time he had his hair straightened:

> The congolene (hair-straightener) just felt warm when Shorty started combing it in. But then my head caught fire.
>
> I gritted my teeth and tried to pull the sides of the kitchen table together. The comb felt as if it was raking my skin off.
>
> My eyes watered, my nose was running. I couldn't stand it any longer; I bolted to the washbasin. I was cursing Shorty with every name I could think of when he got the spray going and started soap-lathering my head.
>
> He lathered and spray-rinsed, lathered and spray-rinsed, maybe ten or twelve times, each time gradually closing the hot water faucet, with the rinse cold, and that helped some.[21]
>
> This [Malcolm reflected later] was my first really big step toward degradation: when I endured all that pain, literally burning my flesh to have it look like a white man's hair. I had joined that multitude of Negro men and women in America who are so brainwashed into believing that the black people are "inferior" — and white people superior — that they will even violate and mutilate their God-created bodies to try to look "pretty" by white standards.[22]

More important perhaps than the physical mutilation blacks inflict upon themselves trying to ape white characteristics is the psychological and spiritual self-mutilation such efforts require. Sociologist Kenneth Clark tells how early the process begins and how deeply it is ingrained:

> When Negro children as young as three years old are shown white- and Negro-appearing dolls or asked to color pictures of children to look like themselves, many of them tend to reject the dark-skinned dolls as "dirty" and "bad" or to color themselves a light color or a bizarre shade like purple. But the fantasy is not complete, for when asked to identify which doll is like themselves, some Negro children, particularly in the North, will refuse, burst into tears, and run away. By the age of seven most Negro children have accepted the reality that they are, after all, dark-skinned. But the stigma remains; they have been forced to recognize themselves as inferior. Few if any Negroes ever fully lose that sense of shame and self-hatred.[23]

This negative feeling about color is not something that is purely psychological; it has been true since slave days and still is the case that the lighter a Negro's skin (in other words, the more he looks like a white), the better have been his chances for education, higher-paying jobs, and family status. Last summer psychologists at Brandeis and Harvard published the results of a study reaffirming this trend.[24] Thus blackness is an economic burden as well as a psychological one.

Liberal whites may be taken aback by the implication in the statements just quoted that their commitment to the integration of Negroes into "the mainstream" of American life has resulted in the kind of degradation we have seen. Yet this seems to be the case, and its ramifications are far-reaching. It makes comprehensible, for example, what Stokely Carmichael meant in this oft-quoted (and more oft-misquoted) remark:

> Integration has always been Negroes going to white schools because the white schools are good, and black schools are bad. A Negro would go from his school to a better school, a white school. Negroes have been made to believe that everything better is always white. If integration means moving to something white is moving to something better then integration is a subterfuge for white supremacy.[25]

The American Negro *is* different from American whites. He has his own history, centering around the experience of slavery and its effects, and more recently including the rediscovery of his African heritage. The Negro has distinct cultural patterns — patterns of speech, patterns of music and dance, patterns of self-expression and relationship — which may have been produced by this history, but which have outlived it and are now surviving on their own creative energy and integrity. These, like the white ethnic characteristics, will not and should not disappear in the future. It is indeed an insidious "subterfuge for white supremacy" to expect blacks to abandon this heritage as the price, explicit or implicit, for integration via assimilation into America's "mainstream."

> This [insists Mr. Carmichael] is simply neither realistic, nor is it particularly desirable; you can *integrate communities*, but you *assimilate individuals*. Even if such a program were possible, its results would be not to develop the black community as a functional and honorable segment of the total society, with its own cultural identity, life-patterns and institutions, but to abolish it. . . . The fact is that what must be abolished is not the black community but the dependent, colonial status that has been inflicted upon it. The racial and cultural personality of the black community must be preserved and the community must win its liberation while preserving its cultural identity. This is the essential difference between integration, as it is currently practiced, and the concept of Black Power.[26]

The Building of Pride

As this treatment of current concepts of integration suggests, the spokesmen for Black Power see their first task as that of producing a sense of individual and group pride among American Negroes in their identity as a distinct cultural entity. This is logical because a self-image of inferiority was originally instilled in Negroes as one means of keeping them resigned to slavery. Kenneth Stampp wrote that a basic step toward successful slave management

> . . was to implant in the bondsmen themselves a consciousness of personal inferiority. They had "to know and keep

their places," to "feel the difference between master and slave," to understand that bondage was their natural status. They had to feel that African ancestry tainted them, that their color was a badge of degradation.[27]

The slave-owners and their successors did a good job. They succeeded, as Kenneth Clark has documented,[28] in making the mass of Negroes to this day consider themselves inferior because of their color, and thus to suspect that a racist social order is somehow coherent with the nature of things. Anyone who has worked in the South attempting to register Negroes knows that his first problem is not facing the white registrars and deputies, but convincing black people that the right to vote is *for them* a legitimate aspiration. The exponents of Black Power believe they must persuade Negroes that to be conscious and proud of their color and its culture, and to expect to struggle for "integration" into American society on that basis, not only *is* a legitimate aspiration, but that it is indeed the *first* legitimate aspiration of a free people.

To begin an attack on this sense of inferiority, Negroes must realize that their oppression is a group phenomenon and not an individual one. This is a persistent theme of Carmichael's:

> The history of every institution of this society indicates that a major concern in the ordering and structuring of the society has been the maintaining of the black community in its condition of dependence and oppression. This has not been on the level of *individual* acts of discrimination between individual whites and individual blacks, but as *total acts* by the white community against the black community. This fact cannot be too strongly emphasized. . . .[29]

> . . . Black people in this country are oppressed for one reason — and that's because of their color . . . their rally cry must be the issue around which they are oppressed, as it was for unions. The workers came together, they were oppressed because they were workers. And we must come together around the issue that oppressed us— which is our blackness. Unions — they needed power to stop their oppression. We need power to stop ours. So it's black power. And black power just means black people coming together and getting people to represent their needs and to stop that oppression.[30]

From birth, black people are told a set of lies about themselves. We are told that we are lazy — yet I drive through the Delta area of Mississippi and watch black people picking cotton in the hot sun for fourteen hours. We are told, "if you work hard, you'll succeed" — but if that were true, black people would own this country. We are oppressed because we are black — not because we are ignorant, not because we are lazy, not because we're stupid (and got good rhythm), but because we're black.[31]

Even our common slang vocabulary abounds with pejorative associations of blackness: blackball; things look black; blackmail; blackguard; blacklist; black book; Black Thursday (Friday, Monday); black-hearted; black magic; black mark; black market; Black Hand; black lie (opposed to "white lie"); a covert CIA operation is "black"; etc.

The first blow to be struck against white supremacy and its effects on the Negro personality is for blacks to begin acting *for themselves as a group* in the context of their racial and cultural identity. This is a position no present major civil rights groups except CORE and SNCC have taken in public. Other, more "moderate," organizations, though mostly black-controlled, depend for their resources on whites and thus dare not project such a stance.

The position of Dr. Martin Luther King, Jr. is that of a center figure speaking from within the Negro community but operating on a strategy designed to make use of characteristics common to all Americans (religion, the law, the Constitution, etc.) as levers for change. The motto of Dr. King's Southern Christian Leadership Conference is, significantly, "Redeeming the Soul of America." This center strategy is, it would seem, legitimate and even necessary in the Negro struggle. But Black Power's attempt to create solidarity and dignity *within* the black community itself is also legitimate — distinct from, but not incompatible with, the reconciling efforts of Dr. King. Perhaps this is why King's statements on Black Power have been ambiguous and hedged, not accepting the idea wholly but not rejecting it totally either.[32] Present-day discussions and events seem to suggest continuing tension between the two approaches within a basic coexistence.

The task of getting blacks to act *as blacks,* by themselves and *for themselves,* is the task of developing "black consciousness" or "psychological equality":

> Black people can and should develop what we have in our own neighborhood and make it good and beautiful. It's time for some psychological equality. To a Negro, faith in himself plus power equals black power.[33]

The necessity for blacks to act in their own communities for themselves leads logically to the policy that organizers in Negro communities ought to be Negro. Thus Carmichael:

> The need for psychological equality is the reason why SNCC today believes that blacks must organize in the black community. Only black people can convey the revolutionary idea that black people are able to do things themselves.... In the past, white allies have furthered white supremacy without the whites realizing it — or wanting it, I think....[34]

Mr. L. A. Vyas, of the Lovedale School, Nilgiris, South India, a veteran of the later phases of his country's struggle for independence, has pointed out to me that in this respect of seeing the development of group pride and self-reliance as its first task, Black Power is not unlike the program of Gandhi. When the Mahatma began his campaigns, there was a group of half-breed Anglo-Indians who resembled the American black bourgeoisie in many respects. They referred to themselves as "British" (though the British never considered them their peers); they talked of England as "home," though few had ever been there. They spoke English, dressed in British styles, aped British manners, professed Christianity, and referred to Indians with the equivalent of "Nigger." Many full-blooded Indians actually felt themselves inferior to their rulers.

Gandhi fought this "slave mentality" in many ways. He called for the use of local languages in the Indian universities. He initiated the Swadeshi movement, which urged the people to reject British imports and to use instead goods produced in their own country, even if they were more expensive or of not as high quality. This was also the basis for Gandhi's insistence on wearing the coarse, homespun clothing of India's poor. He also adopted the wearing of a prisoner's cap, both as a symbolic protest against the national incarceration that was Imperial rule, and as a form of Indian self-identification and solidarity.

If we mentally transplant such tactics to our own country, we conjure up a vision that suspiciously resembles Marcus Garvey's "Buy Black" slogans, the Muslims' rejection of "slave names" for the X which represents their lost tribal names, and — yes — Black Power's call for "black consciousness" and "psychological equality." I am not attempting to make Messrs. Carmichael or McKissick into latter-day Gandhis; but it seems clear that the Mahatma would understand and even sympathize with a strategy that called for group solidarity and pride as a prerequisite to an effective struggle for liberation.

The strategic — as distinct from the psychological — implications of Negro group pride and solidarity reduce to the proposition, stated implicitly above, that because America's blacks have been oppressed as a group, any effective action to end this oppression must be initiated by Negroes as a self-conscious, autonomous group, supported by Negroes and led by representatives that are directly responsible to such a solidly Negro community. This is the meaning of the phrase "independent political action":

> In such areas as Lowndes [County, Alabama] where black men have a majority, they will attempt to use it to exercise control. This is what they seek: control. Where Negroes lack a majority, Black Power means the creation of power bases from which black people can work to change statewide or nationwide patterns of oppression through pressure from strength — instead of weakness.
>
> Politically, black power means what it has always meant to SNCC: the coming together of black people to elect representatives and to force those representatives to speak to their needs.[35]

The need for leadership responsible to the Negro community is the reason SNCC rejects the Democratic Party. SNCC believes the Democratic machines have prevented black people from controlling their own communities, especially in the Northern cities. Carmichael is vehement about this rejection:

> The Democratic Party in this country is the most treacherous enemy of the Negro period. We've got to split it so Johnson and all the king's horses and all the king's men can't put it together again. The only way the Negro in Alabama will get justice is to smash the Democratic Party.
>
> And the national party is opposed to the interests of Negroes. The Daley machine in Chicago is the same thing as the Wallace machine in Alabama. The Negroes in Watts are all loyal Democrats, and they're not going to get anything until they get out of the Democratic Party. And we've got to start tearing up the Democratic Party in Harlem.
>
> We're trying to get power. The power structure doesn't want black people to have power. I'm not talking about George Wallace, I'm talking about Bobby Kennedy. They don't want black people to have power. It's in the interests of Robert Kennedy and Washington to squash [such organizations as] the Lowndes County Freedom Organization because it will spread. And that's what we're working for. A national alternative, when Negroes will be organized independently, neither Republican nor Democrat. So it's in their interests to stop us.[36]

The Democratic Party's strength has been forged through a coalition of Southern forces with the big-city machines. The Southern wing of the party, fully as much as the formal opposition Republicans, has been the major obstacle to the enactment and enforcement of effective civil rights legislation. The movement's concentration before 1966 on Southern resistance to Negro demands provided a valuable smoke screen for the monumental indifference and hypocrisy of the Northern urban Democratic forces. But with the riots of 1965 and 1966, and the open-housing campaign of Dr. King in Chicago during the latter summer, the mask is off the Democrats' northern base as well.[37]

It is clear that the party of Roosevelt has been a major accomplice in the creation and perpetuation of the explosive urban ghettoes which now contain most of America's Negro population. Democrats like the former Senator Paul Douglas of Illinois, who during his last campaign courageously and publicly reaffirmed his support for open-housing legislation even when speaking in Chicago's lily-white suburbs, must be regarded as signal — and inspiring — exceptions.[38] Most Democratic Negro office-holders are mere appendages of the machines, whose function has been largely, in Carmichael's term, that of "vote deliverers"[39] for the machines rather than representatives of organized black constituencies.

DESPAIR: A CONSTANT SHADOW

Tension underlies the calls of Black Power advocates for Negro pride and group action; it flickers between the lines of most of their statements. This tension is between their articulations and policies of hope and their experience of a national and world situation that seems increasingly hopeless. This feeling is not the comfortable melancholy of the "alienated" middle-class intellectual; it is a gut-feeling resulting from direct involvement in a social system that seems bent on their personal and collective destruction.

Kenneth Clark suggests one component of such a feeling:

> With the growth of the civil rights movement, Negroes have won many footholds earlier forbidden them, and it would seem logical to conclude, as many do, that Negroes are better off than ever before in this gradually desegregating and generally affluent society. But the fact is that in many ways the Negro's situation is deteriorating. The Negro has been left out of the swelling prosperity and social progress of the nation as a whole. He is in danger of becoming a permanent economic proletariat.[40]

Another major component is the violence, both institutional and personal, to which Negroes are subjected, both North and South. James Farmer notes

> ... the resentment Negroes feel over the way whites swarm over them with criticism the moment they abandon pure love and merely consider the notion of self-defense. The hypocrisy of this criticism is galling. The Negro sees analogies everywhere. There was silence in the press during the years in which hundreds of thousands of Congolese were being slaughtered; but then there came huge headlines: FIFTY WHITES KILLED IN CONGO. Why not an airlift to Mississippi, they ask?[41]

Police protection for Negroes is largely nonexistent in the South, and visible in the North primarily as the instrument of oppression. The story told by Robert (Moses) Parris, Director of SNCC's 1964 Mississippi Summer Project, evokes this reality of the Negro's world:

> In Talahatchee County [Mississippi] last winter [1964] a Negro shot a policeman. The policeman was messing with him and he shot him. Now he went home, and immediately they organized a vigilante group, maybe a hundred people or more. They had machine guns, rifles, automatics.... They went to this guy's house and they shot it up plank by plank and they dismembered him. They started at the bottom plank and they went all the way up. You have to ask yourself, "What happens to Negroes who know what would happen to a Negro who considers arming himself to do violence to other whites?"[42]

Walter Palmer, a Black Power worker in Philadelphia (Pa.), sums the situation up thus:

> The white person's death is not always as near to him as mine is to me; mine is very close to me all the time.[43]

And James Baldwin has said:

> The brutality with which Negroes are treated in this country simply cannot be overstated, however unwilling white men may be to hear it. In the beginning — and neither can this be overstated — a Negro just cannot *believe* that white people are treating him as they do; he does not know what he has done to merit it. And when he realizes that the treatment accorded him has nothing to do with anything he has done, that the attempt of white people to destroy him — for that is what it is — is utterly gratuitous, it is not hard for him to think of white people as devils.[44]

It is these forces which leave the Black Power movement hovering near despair. Its advocates are certain that American blacks must assert their manhood, their humanity; but they are not at all certain that blacks *can* assert their manhood and survive. It is not difficult to find whites who will reinforce this apprehension. Witness the following exchange between James Meredith, Carmichael, and reporter Lawrence Spivak on NBC's *Meet the Press:*

Mr. Meredith: ... now you take Mississippi, for instance — I know the people that shot in my house years ago. They know the people that killed all of the Negroes that have been killed. The community knows them; the whites know them, and the Negroes know them, and I am here to say that these people have to be removed from our society. White supremacy will not allow itself to remove these people from its society. If they don't find a way, the Negro has no choice but to remove these men, and they have to be removed. You can't have killers running around in the society killing people themselves.

Mr. Spivak: Are you suggesting then that if several Negroes are killed or any white men are killed and the law does not punish them, as happens very often in the case of white men too, that people ought to organize as vigilantes and go out and take the law into their own hands and commit violence? You are not saying that, are you, Mr. Meredith?

Mr. Meredith: That is exactly what I am saying. Exactly.

Mr. Carmichael: If you don't want us to do it, who is going to do it?

Mr. Meredith: I know personally the man who tried to kill my family when I was at the University of Mississippi, and everybody in the community knows him. I know that in all of the other communities in Mississippi—and you have read about all these killings — during the march they killed this 65-year-old (Negro) man, shot him 16 times, shot his head off.

Mr. Spivak: But you didn't pick up a gun and go out and try to kill that man because the law hadn't taken care of him; you don't believe in that, do you?

Mr. Meredith: This is what we are going to have to move to. If the law doesn't take these men, then we've got to stop this. We cannot continue to tolerate this. Now I know why —

Mr. Spivak: Mr. Meredith, do you mean to tell me that you believe the Negroes in this country ought to organize, take up guns and if the law doesn't take care of the wrongs that the white man or other Negroes commit against him, they ought to take the law into their own hands?

Mr. Meredith: This is precisely, and I will tell you why, because the white supremacy is a system —

Mr. Spivak: Mr. Meredith, this doesn't even make sense against 180 million people. If you do it, they are going to do it.[45]

Mr. Spivak's incredulous response to what Meredith was saying dramatically shows the gap between white and Negro experience in American society. The reporter overlooked one crucial fact when he said, "If you do it, they are going to do it," namely, the fact that the whites *are* doing it and *have been* doing it for generations with virtual impunity. Three times in the exchange Meredith and Carmichael hedged their assertions with "If the law does not deal with these men . . .; or asked, "If you don't want us to do it, who is going to do it?" Spivak did not respond to these qualifications, and neither has white society responded to these questions as they have been raised by all the outraged and sorrowing Negro victims of white violence. The best the whites seem able to do is to refer Negroes to a legal process that is at best patchy, cumbersome, expensive, slow, and at worst — and it is usually at its worst in the Negro's situation — no recourse at all. But it is not possible for blacks who must live in constant fear for their safety and the safety of their families to ignore this reality. *They must either submit to it or resist it.*

Another aspect of Mr. Spivak's response that is not an uncommon one is the veiled threat it contains: "If *you* do it, *they* are going to do it." Especially when the speaker is a member of the group that is meant by "they," persons in the "you" group are going to hear threats, as Carmichael pointed out in response:

> . . . we have been forced by statements in this country, which remind us of the 90 percent and what they can do and the 180 million and what they can do — as if they say to us, "Now, if you don't do exactly as we want you to do, if you don't follow what we prescribe for you, then we have the power to wipe you out." That threat is not going to stand in my mind as a black man. . . .[46]

Carmichael refuses, as he feels a man *must* refuse, to be intimidated by what he can't help but hear in Mr. Spivak's (and white society's) statements. In fact he feels it necessary to reject the threat in kind:

> . . . I am a little bit tired of that 90 percent theory. . . . While we may be ten percent inside the country . . . we want to

make it crystal clear that we are well located in cities across this country and that if in fact 180 million people just think they are going to turn on us and we are going to sit there, like the Nazis did to the Jews, they are wrong. We are going to go down together, all of us.[47]

Now the terms of the confrontation are unmistakable: Black Power says to Negroes that they must assert their manhood, and part of manhood is meeting and stopping the kind of violence that Negroes have been subjected to in our society. If the law does not protect blacks, which it has, in fact, not done for the most part, then they must protect *themselves*. If white society chooses, as is implied in statements like Mr. Spivak's, to use Negroes' efforts at self-defense as an excuse for mass violence against blacks, then the blacks will die fighting in a final assertion of their manhood.

Such feelings are not all words. Kenneth Clark describes the tone and feeling of Negro youths during the Harlem riots of 1964:

> You cannot hear the conversations of a mob, but during the disturbance in Harlem, groups of young people discussed their plans: "I'll go home and come back tomorrow. Whitey will still be here." "I don't want to be killed tonight; tomorrow will be all right." There was an eerie, surrealistic quality, a silence within the din, punctuated by gunfire and sporadic shattering of glass, a calm within the chaos, a deliberateness within the hysteria. The Negro seemed to say, during those days of social despair, "We have had enough. The only weapon you have is bullets. The only thing you can do is to kill us." Paradoxically, his apparent lawlessness was a protest against lawlessness directed against *him*. His acts were a desperate assertion of his desire to be treated *as a man*. He was affirmative up to the point of inviting death; he insisted upon being visible and understood. If this was the only way to relate to society at large, he would die rather than be ignored.[48]

James Jackson, a young Watts resident, movingly tells a similar story in a poem written after his ghetto's explosion in 1965:

> I'm here. At least I'm here.
> Despite the bitter pain and fear,
>   I'm here.

> I cry. I smile. I'm here.
> Mother Earth, I'm **here**.[49]

Clearly, Black Power sees violence as a last resort, something to be considered only when other alternatives are not available. "In movements," Carmichael told the *Christian Science Monitor,* "you decide either to be guerillas or you decide not to use violence. We are aggressively nonviolent. But if we are attacked, we are certainly going to move to destroy the persons who attack us."[50] The Black Power programs of independent organization are alternatives to violence. But there is no question that Carmichael and SNCC are uncertain, if not pessimistic, about their chances of success:

> For example [Carmichael told a questioner], my good friend Julian Bond, he's been elected (to the Georgia House of Representatives) three times, and they won't let him sit down [The Supreme Court has since ruled that the Georgia House's refusal to seat Bond violated his rights of free speech, and he has been seated]. So the question is what are the alternatives? And what is this country going to do about that? It's clear to me that if there are no alternatives once one goes through the legal structures then there must be some kind of change. And we're going through these legal processes. The question is whether or not the majority of people in this country, who are white Americans, are they ever going to make this country a real democracy? 'Cause that's where the problem really lies. The question is, can white people move in and change the institutions of this country to allow for people to live as human beings in this country?[51]

SNCC's Chairman was less circumspect in discussing the Lowndes County Freedom Party's political campaign in the summer and fall of 1966:

> We're out to take power legally, but if we're stopped by the government from doing it legally, we're going to take it the way everyone else took it including the way Americans took it in the American Revolution. And we've seen the way the federal government protects us, or rather doesn't protect us. If one of our candidates gets touched, we're going to take care of the murderers ourselves.[52]

The defeat of the Lowndes County Freedom Party at the polls in November 1966 came through Negro votes, not in spite of them: too many fearful Negro voters cast their ballots under the watchful eyes of their white plantation landlords. This suggests that the Party will not consider its organizing job as completed, and thus not all alternatives closed off.[53]

One cannot reasonably say that the elections of 1966 gave Negroes much ground for hope. An individual victory such as that of Republican Senator Edward Brooke of Massachusetts (whose election Carmichael specifically rejected as in any sense a "Negro" victory, because of the overwhelming white majority among the electorate which sent Brooke to Washington[54]), was overshadowed by the gains of conservative Republicans in the House, a development that has re-established the GOP-Southern Democrat coalition that stalled progressive legislation for decades. Black Power groups have become very skeptical, in any case, about the value of legislation, as we will see in the next chapter. Lincoln Lynch, Associate Director of CORE, told an interviewer of this disillusionment:

> Wonderful things have been promised, even by the President. But we black people don't believe them anymore. We don't believe them anymore. What are you telling me, you're having a war on poverty! They've passed a $58 billion defense budget. And they're arguing over whether they will pass a $2 billion anti-poverty act.
>
> That is the sort of thing we're talking about; the gap between what is said and what is done — between promise and performance.[55]

SNCC's pessimism about social change as a live alternative to holocaust is not limited to domestic affairs, as its Chairman has stated:

> For a century this nation has been like an octopus of exploitation, its tentacles stretching from Mississippi and Harlem to South America, the Middle East, Southern Africa and Vietnam; the form of exploitation varies from area to area but the essential result has been the same — a powerful few have been maintained and enriched at the expense of the poor and voiceless colored masses.[56]

SNCC believes that, to be true to its heritage and mission, the black community must tie its liberation struggle to the struggle of other oppressed nonwhite peoples around the world. This is the basis for their rejection of proposals like the "Freedom Budget" outlined by the A. Philip Randolph Institute[57] and endorsed by most "mainstream" Negro and white liberal leaders. The aim of the Freedom Budget is to wipe out poverty in the United States by redistributing the national income; but it proposes to do so, SNCC charges, without asking where the income is coming from. Because much of the wealth to abolish poverty would come from U.S. exploitation of non-white people in Africa and elsewhere, SNCC feels that such a plan could only succeed in making American Negroes full partners in a system of international racism, enabling them to live well off the sweat of their black brothers on other continents. SNCC rejects this as a betrayal of the struggle, and will have none of it.[58]

But thus isolated from traditional supporters of the civil rights movement, how can a Black Power movement hope to mobilize the political forces necessary to change this system? "For racism to die," Stokely Carmichael declares, "a totally different America must be born."[59] But who will be the midwife? Bayard Rustin has pointed out that even if all the American poor — black and white — could be welded into one organization, which is the only coalition SNCC has said it considers realistic, they would still be nowhere near a majority of the population, and could not hope to win an all-out political confrontation.[60] But where this leads Rustin to conclude that the movement must seek middle-class "liberal" allies, with whom compromises like the Freedom Budget must be made, SNCC can only admit that there may indeed be *no* real allies for their struggle. Moreover, they fully expect the system to respond to such a basic challenge as Black Power implies at home in the same ways it responds (remember Mr. Spivak's remark) to challenges in South Africa, Cuba, Santo Domingo, and of course Vietnam. In such an eventuality, Black Power people will go down fighting.

This tension, this near-despair is, as we suggested, widespread among Negroes generally, and it is growing more intense. Rev. James Breeden, a Negro staff member of the

National Council of Churches Commission on Religion and Race, told a Valley Forge audience: "We are very close in this country to having to decide whether to commit *genocide* — and I'm not using that word symbolically — or to mobilize the resources of the nation to produce something approximating social justice."[61] James Baldwin told fellow novelist Budd Schulberg in a conversation recorded by *Playboy* magazine:

> Our children are being murdered. This has been very much on my mind, I didn't realize how much. And some of us have been trying — despairingly — to figure out what to do to save at least a remnant on that day when we are forced to realize that there is no hope for us here, no hope at all. As far as I am concerned, when my countrymen can set dogs on children and blow children up in Sunday school, the holocaust is not far off. And, more than that — if I'm to be honest — one can't but feel, no matter how deeply one distrusts the feeling, that the holocaust, the total leveling, salvation by fire, "no remission of sins save by the shedding of blood," may be the only hope.[62]

To talk about genocide in America may seem like utter hogwash to white liberals, but only if they have forgotten their own history. White America *is* indeed capable of genocide; we have already committed it. Ask any American Indian.

BLACK POWER AND BLACK CRITICS

Some of the fiercest attacks on Black Power have come from widely known and distinguished figures within the Negro community. Such attacks deserve a more respectful hearing than do the criticisms of most whites, which can always be suspected of misunderstanding or simply dismissed as racist euphemism. The fact that the criticisms made by such Negro figures closely parallel those made by liberal whites only makes an examination of them more appropriate.

Representative Negro critiques of Black Power have been made by Roy Wilkins, Executive Secretary of the NAACP; by Carl Rowan, former USIA director and Ambassador to Finland; by Dr. Samuel Du Bois Cook, a professor of political science at Atlanta University; and by Bayard Rustin, Director of the A. Philip Randolph Institute.[63] The first three can be considered together. Their indictment of Black Power reduces to the charge that it is a call for Negro racism and/or separatism. Dr. Cook states this clearly:

> Shorn of pretension, hyprocrisy, and intellectual dishonesty, the slogan "Black Power" does have, when words, context, and program are combined, a generic or core meaning, and that meaning is racist. It is anti-white. It is separatist and isolationist. Make no mistake about it: vigorous denials under pressure notwithstanding, the unique dimension of the Black Power myth is racism.[64]

Roy Wilkins has expressed his sentiments with equal strength:

> No matter how endlessly they try to explain it, the term "Black Power" means anti-white power.
> Ideologically, it dictates "up with black and down with white" in precisely the same fashion that South Africa reverses that slogan.
> It is a reverse Mississippi, a reverse Hitler, a reverse Ku Klux Klan.[65]

Rowan cites Wilkins as having

> blasted the policies of racial isolation that the "Black Power" advocates are pushing by saying: Negroes are Americans, citizens of the United States; their identity is here, as Americans. Separatism isn't going to get us very far. It is exotic and a little intoxicating, but it lacks the reality that 99% of Negro Americans must face each day....[66]

Rowan himself writes quite confidently of the separatist intentions of Black Power's leading spokesmen:

> ...I recognize the old "separate but equal" argument when I hear it. I've read *Plessy vs. Ferguson* more times than I've read Carmichael's name, and I've argued with enough Deep South governors and politicians who favored separation of the races, to recognize what appears to be an appeal to the Negro's pride but is in fact an effort to flatter black men into believing that the short end of the stick is really the fat of Willie Mays' bat. Generations of enforced isolation of the Negro proved that "there ain't no such animal" as separate but equal; and voluntary isolation of the Negro isn't going to produce any such animal.
> [Stokely] Carmichael and [Floyd McKissick] are not the first to preach black separatism, of course. Marcus Garvey

wanted to haul all Negroes back to Africa. The Communist Party once promised Negroes the whole state of Mississippi.[67]

Of the consequences of Black Power's alleged racism-separatism, three of the most offensive to these black liberals are what they see as its rejection of integration, nonviolence, and Negro-white coalitions. Rowan says:

> The Black Power advocates ... created a crisis of leadership within the civil rights movement.... This raised what is still the crucial question: does the Negro seek integration within the mainstream of American society, which admittedly will be difficult to attain; or black supremacy, which common sense says is impossible to achieve; or a separatism that would give black Americans special enclaves in which they can exercise total Power ...? Negroes must [also] decide whether whites are to be ousted from the civil rights movement.[68]

Dr. Cook is more sweeping:

> The racist character of the myth of Black Power is expressed in many ways: counsel to exclude whites from positions of leadership and influence in the civil rights movement, advocacy of independent all-Negro third parties, the symbol of the Black Panther, the call for a "black takeover of political and economic power," the declaration of the irrelevance of integration and the issue of violence, self-righteous and glib assertions of the moral decadence of white America, and the general ventilations of anti-white frustrations, emotions and bitterness.[69]

And Wilkins:

> There has now emerged, first a strident and threatening challenge to a strategy widely employed by civil rights groups, namely non-violence.
>
> If carried out literally as instant retaliation, in cases adjudged by aggrieved persons to have been grossly unjust, this policy could produce — in extreme situations — lynchings or, in better-sounding phraseology, private vigilante vengeance.
>
> [And further]: Though it be clarified and clarified again, "Black Power" in the quick, uncritical and highly emotional adoption it has received from segments of a beleaguered people can mean in the end only black death.[70]

That these objections are virtually indistinguishable from

the comments opposing Black Power that have appeared in the liberal white press, can be seen from the following quotations, the first from *The New York Times:*

> Regardless of other interpretations that could reasonably be offered of the term "black power," Mr. Carmichael and his SNCC associates clearly intended to mean Negro nationalism and separatism along racial lines — a hopeless, futile, destructive course expressive merely of a sense of black impotence. As a practical program, it has nothing more to recommend it than the wretched violence that some Chicago whites have been using in recent days against the Rev. Dr. Martin Luther King and his Negro followers.
>
> Effective politics for Negroes, as for any other group, means bringing pressure to bear at the right times and places and taking part in shifting alliances with other groups.
>
> But most of the militants who make up SNCC and CORE have no taste or talent for the arduous practice of sophisticated politics. They are taking refuge from the hard fact of the dwindling effectiveness of direct action by escaping into black nationalism.[71]

In the next comment, James Wechsler, editor and columnist for *The New York Post,* who considers himself solidly committed to the Negro cause, makes plain his objections to Black Power:

> It is an affront, even a form of racism, when [Carmichael's] stale and sterile manifestoes are heralded in some liberal salons as the preachings of a prophet; in fact he is being patronized, just as poor Malcolm X was in his heyday. . . .
>
> This is the politics of either desperation or demagogy. If it be assumed that men who have served so resolutely in the fronts lines of a hundred civil rights battles must now be branded inferiors because their skin is white, all concept of coalition is dead. This I am unprepared to concede.
>
> In too many areas, the spirit of separation — most crudely expressed in the slogan "black power" — has become an excuse for the reaffirmation of primitive intolerances in the white community.
>
> But it is one thing to understand the origins of rage in the Negro ghetto; it is another to romanticize their manifestations when they take the form of a new, destructive separatism, preached by men who have seen whites die at their side. . . .
>
> "Integration is a subterfuge for the maintenance of

white supremacy," wrote Stokely Carmichael . . . thereby in a sentence proposing to reverse the whole thrust of the effort for which Negroes and whites have hand in hand exposed themselves to the fire and fury of the racists. . . .

. . . It has to be stated bluntly that the raising of the slogan of "black power" was a diversionary disaster. It was as foolish, self-defeating, and irrelevant as the chant of "self-determination for the black belt," advanced by the Communist Party in the early 1930's in its desperate effort to imitate and apply the tactics of the Russian Bolsheviks to the American landscape. . . .[72]

In both of these pieces we hear pretty much the same refrain as before: charges of racism, separatism, violence, rejection of integration and coalitions.

How valid are these criticisms? Our previous discussion of the elements and mood of Black Power provides the framework for an evaluation of them. Stokely Carmichael and other spokesmen have repeatedly replied to charges very similar to these, and we will cite them as our witnesses.

Are, then, racism and separatism concomitants of Black Power? None of the three authors pauses to define either term, but it is apparent that they use racism as meaning black supremacy. Separatism means something very close to a Garveyesque back-to-Africa program, or to what the Communists advocated in the 30's or the Black Muslims advocate today — one or more separate states for blacks. Dr. Cook speaks of racism thus, "Black Power, or domination, is a dangerous myth and self-defeating illusion."[73] *The Crisis,* Wilkins' NAACP magazine, editorially equated the new slogan with racism by asserting: "In a pluralistic society, the slogan 'black power' is as unacceptable as 'white supremacy'."[74]

It is safe to say that none of these charges speak to the concept of Black Power as enunciated by SNCC and CORE. Carmichael remarked to a Massachusetts audience:

The standard argument represented against independent political organizations is: "But you are only 10%." I cannot see what the relevance of this observation is, since no one is talking about taking over the country but taking control of our own communities.[75]

This remark is consistent with the intentions of Black Power that we cited earlier. Carmichael elaborated on this theme in *The New York Review of Books:*

> Black people do not want to "take over" this country. They don't want to "get whitey"; they just want him off their backs, as the saying goes. . . . The white man is irrelevant to blacks, except as an oppressive force. Blacks want to be in his place, yes, but not in order to terrorize and lynch and starve him. They want to be in his place because that is where a decent life can be had.[76]

These sentiments square with what Mr. Carmichael tells Negro audiences. He exhorted a crowd in Greenwood, Mississippi, during the Meredith March, telling them:

> You must build a power base . . . the power base has to get you a black sheriff . . . white people aren't going to do it for you . . . you have to stop being ashamed of being black and don't try to be white. . . . Now that doesn't mean to be anti-white . . . but get the nappiest headed black man with the broadest nose and the thickest lips and make him sheriff.[77]

In *Ebony* magazine, as elsewhere, Carmichael has insisted that "Black Power doesn't mean that we are anti-white, it means that we are too busy tending to our real work, organizing poor black people, to worry about white people."[78] Similar themes run through reports of his speeches to Negro audiences in Harlem, Newark, Detroit, and Watts.[79]

There is no evidence in the thrust of black consciousness to support charges of racism. To take charge of one's own personal and group destiny does not have to imply a desire for ascendency for that group over all others — though with the obstacles faced by black people in America today, such an effort is not likely to come to fruition, it seems to me, without some friction between groups. Still, there remains a fundamental difference in kind between the ethnic pride evident in the St. Patrick's Day Parades in New York, or Gandhi's Swadeshi campaign, or black consciousness, and the monstrous bigotry that was ingrained in Hitler's Jungvolk thirty years ago. It is sheer nonsense to compare Black Power with Hitler

or South Africa, as did Roy Wilkins. It is erroneous to allege,
as did Dr. Cook, that SNCC is planning, or even hoping for,
a "black takeover of political and economic power." Dr. Cook
places quotation marks around that phrase, but fails to give a
source for it: I have not found one like it in the fairly ex-
tensive literature I have surveyed, and I feel safe in suggesting that in that reference Dr. Cook let his emotion get
the better of his scholarship.

Rowan expands his charge of separatism by way of a
"homely" figure of speech:

> The Negro has said for generations: "We don't aim to
> lick the white man, but we sure intend to join him — in the
> enjoyment of every blessing of American life." Admittedly he
> is having one hell of a time joining the white man at the
> banquet. But he's got one leg under the table. Now SNCC
> and CORE are saying, "If we join the white man he'll lick
> us." So they want the Negro to run off to what will be a
> crumb-laden table in a cranny off the kitchen, plaster up a
> sign saying "black power," and pretend that the black man
> has found paradise.[80]

Rowan is, of course, ignoring here the basic political assertion of Black Power, which has not been a matter of
whether the Negro wants to join the white man "at the banquet," but a matter of *how* and on *what basis* he is to join
the white man "at the banquet." Carmichael addressed this
criticism when he asserted:

> The single aspect of the Black Power program which has
> come into the most criticism is the concept of independent
> organization. This is represented as third-partyism, which has
> never worked, or a withdrawal into black nationalism and
> isolationism. If such a program is done, it will not have the
> effect of isolating the black community, but the reverse. When
> the black community is able to control local office, and ne-
> gotiate with other groups from a position of organized
> strength, the possibility of *meaningful* political alliances on
> specific issues will be increased. That is a rule of politics, and
> there is no reason why it should not operate here. The only
> difference is that we will have the power to define the terms
> of our alliances.[81]

This seems to be a realistic and nonseparatist view of

how to win Negroes their proper plateful at Rowan's "banquet." Black Power only insists that "the community must win its liberation while preserving its cultural identity."[82] It is fair to say that Black Power would dissent from Rowan's statement that the Negro has even "one leg under the table"; it would probably find more congenial to its view of the Negro's situation the comparison made by Malcolm X: "The black American today shows us the perfect parasite image — the black tick under the delusion that he is progressing because he rides the udder of the fat, three-stomached cow that is white America."[83]

The charge of racism by exclusion of whites also holds little water. A SNCC internal paper leaked to *The New York Times* (to SNCC's chagrin but to the careful reader's benefit), discussed candidly, and not for public gaze, the analysis underlying the shift in its policy:

> What we have now [in SNCC before Black Power] is a closed society. A clique. Black people cannot relate to SNCC, because of its unrealistic, nonracial atmosphere; denying their experience of America as a racist society.
>
> If we are to proceed toward true liberation, we [SNCC] must cut ourselves off from white people. We must form our own institutions, credit unions, co-ops, political parties, write our own histories. . . .
>
> These facts do not mean that whites cannot help. They can participate on a voluntary basis. We can contract work out to them, but in no way can they participate on a policy-making level.
>
> The charge may be made that we are "racists," but whites who are sensitive to our problems will realize that we must determine our own destiny.[84]

Judging by their remarks the critics of Black Power do not seem to grasp how literally the SNCC demand for blacks to organize their own institutions is an extension of their basic determination truly to control their own destinies. Nor do the critics seem to comprehend the difficulty of establishing even a small but visible black island in the white American sea. This is the problem SNCC's working paper was grappling with, in an effort to avoid the suffocation of assimilation. It does not seem likely that SNCC has overestimated the obstacles to a visible Negro cultural identity. C. Eric Lincoln, who studied the Black Muslims, has remarked provocatively that

> "American" . . . has an implication of color. Few of us have really lost the feeling that this is a "white man's country" and that all other races enjoy it by the white man's sufferance. We do not say this bluntly: it is considered in poor taste and, if quoted abroad, not in the national interest. Our text-books, mass media and community behavior confirm this white nationalism everywhere.[85]

Silberman also speaks of the pervasiveness of color associations:

> . . . [Negro] children become aware almost from infancy of the opprobrium Americans attach to color. . . . They become aware of it as they begin to watch television, or go to the movies, or read the mass-circulation magazines; beauty, success, and status all wear a white skin. They learn to feel ashamed of their color as they learn to talk, and thereby to absorb the invidiousness our very language attaches to color.[86] White represents purity and goodness; black represents evil.[87]

It is undeniable, and not really surprising, that our national self-images and ideals wear white skins; but we can hardly expect black people to find it satisfying. Even where Negroes have managed to get a toehold in the mass media that project these images, they are seen doing the things and exemplifying the characteristics ascribed by a white nation to itself. Even in Negro publications like *Ebony,* the overwhelming majority of models in advertisements have strictly caucasoid features, straight hair and a light complexion. It should not surprise us to hear SNCC talking as if Negroes were choking and gasping for breath in an atmosphere clogged with thick white dust; culturally, such a description is not so far from the truth. Nor should we be surprised to hear SNCC in the same working paper speak thus of finances and staff:

> If we continue to rely upon white financial support we will find ourselves entwined in the tentacles of the white

power complex that controls this country. It is also important that a black organization (devoid of cultism) be projected to our people so that it can be demonstrated that such organizations are viable.[88]

The white power complex referred to is not necessarily a conspiratorial "ruling class," though SNCC, like most of the New Left, regards power in American society as being tightly and increasingly centralized. The phrase implies that, centralized or not, most powerful institutions in this country are controlled by, and expressive of, people whose values and culture blacks find foreign and stifling. Power is monolithic at least in that it is virtually all white, unresponsive to the Negroes' cultural identity and even destructive of it.[89] Thus, if Negroes are seriously hoping to preserve their group identity, they must create and develop institutions that will be responsive to and expressive of that identity. Black control of SNCC, as an organization that is attempting to articulate this form of cultural self-preservation, is fundamental if SNCC's message is to have credibility among black people. The mass of Negroes must be able to see a black-run group running its own affairs, defining its own strategies, carrying out its own programs — and even making its own mistakes. While it is true that most whites have left SNCC, its Executive Committee still has a white member, the staff of the New York office and several project staffs are still interracial. The worst that SNCC can be in fact convicted of is being truly black-controlled. The charges of racist exclusionism raised by Rowan and Cook are beside the point and not actually true.

The matter of SNCC's rejection of nonviolence we have dealt with in some detail earlier.[90] We have seen that it is basically a rejection of nothing except an intolerable situation created by the manifest lack of real protection for life, limb, and property most Negroes must live in. In view of this, suggestions that SNCC and CORE are plotting to install by force of arms some sort of inverted South Africa are simple hogwash. SNCC seems aware that such a determined assertion of the right of self-defense and self-determination is hazardous in a society that has, North and South, deep strains of hostility to

Negro assertions of any sort; but life for most blacks is hazardous enough anyway. And as long as critics who are not also subject to the same conditions do not have an effective, feasible alternative to offer, they can expect to see Negroes defend themselves as they can.

The other major criticism of Black Power is its alleged rejection of a coalition with liberal white forces for political action in the Negro's interest. Because of the ramifications of this objection and Black Power's response to it, and the importance of this dialogue in the thinking of liberal whites, we shall deal with coalition and Black Power in the next chapter.

Chapter Two

THE IDEOLOGY OF THE LIBERAL COALITION

Vice-President Hubert Humphrey, whatever the fickle progressive-radical communities may think of him now, has certainly earned the right to speak as at least a liberal *emeritus*. Those of us in today's "New Left" may have read, before we dropped out of college, of his valiant and lonely battles for the lost cause of civil rights beginning at the 1948 Democratic Convention. Minnesota is not a state where a politician must cater to a large organized Negro population, so the brash freshman Senator's stand could well have been based on that quality we profess to see so little evidenced today, namely, principle. And even the new young radicals can recall that it was the same Hubert Humphrey in 1964 who led the Senate through an exhausting, all-out, last-ditch, bitter-end Southern filibuster to pass the Civil Rights Act. This was perhaps the pinnacle of his career as a fighting liberal, a feat for which he was rewarded with (liberals and radicals would now say "manacled to") the Vice-Presidency.

But two years is a long time, it seems. Now, about the only organization that remembers what went on before is the NAACP (regarded by most radicals as an obstacle to progress), which invited the Vice-President to address its 1966 National Convention. Perhaps there is a kind of poetic justice in the invitation. The Vice-President is a long-time member of the Association, and possibly some of the old-timers in the group, listening to him, remembered the days when even the NAACP was considered radical and left-wing, and members warred bitterly with the likes of entrenched, conservative leaders such as Booker T. Washington.

At the convention Mr. Humphrey seemed a bit more enthusiastic than usual. This was, after all, his old stamping ground. He posed repeatedly for pictures with gaggles of dark children and sundry important association functionaries. And in his speech he was the very incarnation of the grand old coalition of whites and Negroes whose interests he fought for so tirelessly. He sternly rebuked, in diplomatic fashion, his version of Black Power:

> Yes, racism is racism — and there is no room in America for racism of any color. And we must reject calls for racism whether they come from a throat that is white or one that is black.[1]

Then with nostalgia in his voice, the Vice-President spoke feelingly of the long, hard road this coalition had traveled:

> For we marched . . . even when our band was small and our ranks thin and ragged . . . even when victory seemed a distant and unattainable goal.
> There have been young marchers and old . . . Negro and white . . . rich and poor . . . but always marching with a common spirit . . . moved by a common hope — and striving for a common objective.[2]

Mr. Humphrey called for the strengthening of this liberal coalition with allies from business, labor, religious, and community groups and he brought the crowd to its feet when he departed from his prepared text to add, with unmistakable sincerity: *"Do not deny me the chance to be with you."*[3]

This last was a somewhat curious request. It seemed to suggest there were forces that might make it politically impossible for the Vice-President to accept invitations to speak to his old comrades in the civil rights movement. And, of course, Mr. Humphrey's implied apprehensions were quite justified. The next few months saw the 1966 Civil Rights Act defeated, Negro riots in a different city almost every week for the rest of the summer, and an open-housing campaign in

Democratic Chicago resisted with a ferocity even the liberals had not expected. As autumn brought on the election campaigns, Congress, haunted by the specter of the white backlash, began cutting off funds for civil rights enforcement, starving the War on Poverty, and toying with "anti-riot" legislation.

All the while liberal spokesmen, in and out of the Administration, reasserted the importance of the "grand coalition" the Vice-President had spoken of, as the realistic and "responsible" alternative to the new "extremist" cries of Black Power, the latter being usually characterized as racism, calls to violence, etc., etc. We have already heard Roy Wilkins, Carl Rowan, Samuel Cook, and James A. Wechsler vehemently reject the separatism they heard in the new slogan. To these voices may be added two more. George L. P. Weaver, Assistant Secretary of Labor, had this to say in Cleveland:

> Utilizing the law as the vehicle to correct social and economic injustice, and supported by non-violent, brilliantly-conducted protest activities, we achieved necessary court decisions and legislative enactments to provide the framework for improving the status of the American Negro.
>
> But when you attempt [Black Power] you alienate the broad community support of all groups which have been forged together in a common pursuit of justice through ... nonviolence.[4]

A. Philip Randolph, President of the Brotherhood of Sleeping Car Porters and elder statesman of the civil rights movement, writing in a syndicated column, was more specific in his views on the coalition, and more vigorous in his opposition to the new approaches of SNCC and CORE:

> Today, thanks to the monumental sacrifices of the civil rights workers, the support of labor and religious groups, the Negro has at long last won his judicial rights. ...
>
> The reactionary coalition which denies us a substantial minimum wage, which denies us rent subsidies and which diminishes and demeans the war on poverty, can only be smashed by a strong Negro-Labor alliance.[5]

His views on Black Power were succinct:

> Black Power is a menace to racial peace and prosperity.

No Negro who is fighting for civil rights can support Black Power which is opposed to civil rights and integration.[6]

Randolph's views about integration in Negro struggles have changed somewhat over the years. In 1942, while addressing the all-Negro March on Washington Movement, Randolph had some strikingly different — and strangely familiar — things to say:

As to the composition of our movement. Our policy is that it be all Negro, and pro-Negro, but not anti-White, or anti-semitic, or anti-labor, or anti-Catholic. The reason for this policy is that all oppressed people must assume the responsibility and take the initiative to free themselves.

The essential value of an all-Negro movement such as the March on Washington is that it helps to create faith by Negroes in Negroes. It develops a sense of self-reliance with Negroes depending on Negroes in vital matters. It helps to break down the slave psychology and inferiority-complex in Negroes which comes and is nourished with Negroes relying on white people for direction and support. This inevitably happens in mixed organizations that are supposed to be in the interest of the Negro. . . .[7]

What accounts for the apparent shift in Mr. Randolph's thinking is not clear.

RUSTIN ON THE COALITION AND BLACK POWER

Thus far we have heard seven different commentators, white and black, ranging from the highest levels of government to organized labor, the civil rights movement, academic life and journalism, all calling for new or expanded *coalition* efforts as the most effective means of achieving Negro objectives, and as the primary strategy for robbing the Black Power slogan of any appeal to the mass of Negroes. The most detailed, calm, and rational coalitionist critique of Black Power has come from Bayard Rustin, organizer of the 1963 March on Washington and Director of the A. Philip Randolph Institute. His critique appears in two articles — one the now famous "From Protest to Politics,"[8] and the other "Black Power and Coalition Politics."[9] The first article sets forth Rustin's general analysis of the coalition that he sees as being the real cutting edge for Negro liberation. The second essay uses this framework as a basis for the rejection of Black Power.

Rustin bases his strategy on the conviction that the coalition movement has substantially undermined "the elaborate legal structure of segregation and discrimination..."[10] and that it is now faced with the even tougher hurdles of mass poverty, unemployment, slums, and inadequate education that are characteristic of, but not limited to, Negro life today. "At issue," he writes, "is not *civil rights,* strictly speaking, but social and economic conditions. Last summer's [1964] riots were not race riots; they were outbursts of class aggression in a society where class and color definitions are converging disastrously."[11]

This situation, he feels, can only be dealt with through organized political action — undertaken by the familiar coalition:

> Neither the [civil rights] movement nor the country's twenty million black people can win political power alone. We need allies. The future of the Negro struggle depends on whether the contradictions of this society can be resolved by a coalition of progressive forces which becomes the *effective* political majority in the United States. I speak of the coalition which staged the March on Washington, passed the Civil Rights Act, and laid the basis for the Johnson landslide — Negroes, trade unionists, liberals, and religious groups.[12]

For the Negroes to play their full role in this coalition, the movement must "wrest leadership of the ghetto vote from the machines." Only thus can it have "an organized constituency such as other major groups in our society now have."[13] Rustin also points out that the liberal idea of "self-help" must be seen in this perspective:

> Self-help efforts, directly or indirectly, must be geared to mobilizing people into power units capable of effecting social change. That is, their goal must be genuine self-help, not merely self-improvement.[14]

These lines were published before Black Power came on the scene; but in the same article Rustin pauses to lodge objections to what he calls a "no-win" policy espoused by certain militant groups (SNCC, we may infer) who even then appeared skeptical of the coalition approach:

> Sharing with many moderates a recognition of the magnitude of the obstacles to freedom, spokesmen for this tendency survey the American scene and find no forces prepared to move toward racial solutions. From this they conclude that the only viable strategy is shock: above all, the hypocrisy of white liberals must be exposed.... They seek to change white hearts — by traumatizing them.[16]

Rustin feels that these self-appointed "radicals" miss the point:

> Hearts are not relevant to the issue; neither racial affinities nor racial hostilities are rooted there. It is institutions — social, political, and economic institutions — whch are the ultimate molders of collective sentiments. Let these institutions be reconstructed *today*, and let the ineluctable gradualism of history govern the formation of a new psychology.[17]

As he expands his vision of the elements of this coalition, he again decries the "no-win" policy:

> We need to choose our allies on the basis of common political objectives. It has become fashionable in some no-win Negro circles to decry the white liberal as the main enemy (his hypocrisy is what sustains racism)... but the objective fact is that *Eastland and Goldwater* are the main enemies — they and the opponents of civil rights, of the War on Poverty, of Medicare, of social security, of federal aid to education, of unions, and so forth. The labor movement, despite its obvious faults, has been the largest single organized force in this country pushing for progressive social legislation. And where the Negro-labor-liberal axis is weak, as in the farm belt, it was the religious groups that were most influential in rallying support for the Civil Rights Bill.[18]

Rustin is proposing, then, a coalition of "Negroes, trade unionists, liberals, and religious groups"[19] as the primary agency of social change for Negro benefit. His objections to Black Power (in his second article) reduce to a charge that the concept rejects and threatens this coalition. He sees "quasi-nationalistic sentiments and [a] no-win policy lying behind

the slogan which do no service to the Negro."[20] More specifically, he states

> that Black Power not only lacks any real value for the
> civil rights movement, but that its propagation is positively
> harmful. It diverts the movement from a meaningful debate
> over strategy and tactics, it isolates the Negro community,
> and it encourages the growth of anti-Negro forces.[21]

He also attempts to place the emergence of Black Power
in the context of the ghetto experience. To Rustin the slogan
is a reaction to frustration, to "the belief that the ghetto is
destined to last forever."[22] He contends that similar phenomena in the past — Marcus Garvey's Back to Africa movement in the twenties being the outstanding example — produced similar reactions: ". . . with 'Black Power' affording the
same emotional release as 'Back to Africa' and 'Buy Black'
did in earlier periods of frustration and hopelessness."[23]

That Black Power has diverted the movement from
"meaningful debate" on strategy can be best seen, Rustin as-
serts, in furors over the "false issue" of Negro self-defense
versus non-violence, and conflicts over the role of whites in
the movement:

> The reasoning here is that turning the other cheek is
> not the way to win respect, and that only if the Negro suc-
> ceeds in frightening the white man will the white man begin
> to take him seriously. The trouble with this reasoning is
> that it fails to recognize that fear is more likely to bring
> hostility to the surface than respect. . . .[24]

Worse yet, according to Rustin, the emergence of Black Power
has split the civil rights organizations and lost the movement
the moral initiative, permitting "the President and Vice-
President to lecture us about 'racism in reverse' "[25] rather
than addressing the real social and economic issues.

Stokely Carmichael once believed in the coalition approach, says Rustin, but after "countless beatings and 24
jailings [28 at this writing] . . . and the absence of strong and
continual support from the liberal community" the SNCC
Chairman gave up and concluded "that nothing was to be
gained from working with whites, and that an alliance with

the black nationalists was desirable."[26] This is the basis of the "no-win" policy that isolates blacks with a pseudo-strategic dialectic:

> Why bother with programs when their enactment results only in "sham"? Why concern ourselves with the image of the movement when nothing significant has been gained for all the sacrifices made by SNCC and CORE? Why compromise with reluctant white allies when nothing of consequence can be achieved anyway? Why indeed have anything to do with whites at all?[27]

Rustin thus considers Black Power separatist, characterizing it as a "despairing response of the victim" of oppression, which says to the oppressor, "If you don't want me, then I don't want you. . . ." But, unlike the other black critics, Rustin distinguishes this from the racist's declaration — "Whatever you do, I don't want you."[28]

Evidently Rustin has mainly in view his white liberal readers. He believes that Black Power threatens to dilute white support for the Negro struggle:

> It would . . . be tragic if white liberals allowed verbal hostility on the part of Negroes to drive them out of the movement or to curtail their support of civil rights.[29]

Such an attrition, he thinks, has already begun, and it is apparently a major factor in "the growth of anti-Negro forces." This verbal hostility has also made possible "counter-demands for law and order and . . . opposition to police review boards."[30] This trend, the notorious "backlash" (although Rustin does not use that exact term), makes more difficult the task of mobilizing support for the 185-billion dollar "Freedom Budget" proposed by the A. Philip Randolph Institute. SNCC and CORE will be of little help in the coalition effort behind the "Freedom Budget" because "the advocates of 'black power' have no such programs in mind; what they are in fact arguing for (perhaps unconsciously) is the creation of a new black establishment."[31]

Rustin concludes by urging the liberals to defeat Black

Power, not with words but with action — coalition action — to meet the problems giving rise to the slogan.[32]

We may attempt to sum up the coalitionist critique of Black Power thus: the slogan is an unfortunate, though perhaps understandable, response to the increasing frustrations that both ghetto Negroes and civil rights workers have experienced; as a strategy it is unacceptable and impractical because its implicit separatism splits the civil rights movement, ties up civil rights groups in meaningless internal debates over non-violence and integration, and gives the moral initiative to the movement's enemies. All of this, of course, adds up to a threat to the liberal coalition Rustin is counting on to secure the implementation of such programs as the "Freedom Budget."

I have gone into detail to state the coalitionist thesis articulated by Mr. Rustin as objectively as I can. I have done so for several reasons. First, Mr. Rustin's record as a civil rights worker and strategist is long and impressive. Certainly he is entitled to a hearing — the more so because of the relative temperateness of his remarks, a most unusual characteristic of the discussion thus far. Second, the coalitionist strategy underlies the thinking of most whites who, up to now, considered themselves allies of the Negro movement; and so the resolution of the debate is of fundamental importance for the direction liberal thought — and action — is to take, in regard to both the Negro movement and to itself as a movement for directed social change. Third, the concept of Black Power, and the realities on which it is based, necessitate, I believe, a major reinterpretation of the coalition strategy and the role of whites in carrying out such a strategy.

BLACK POWER CHALLENGES THE COALITION

The liberal ideology of the grand coalition can, it seems to me, be formulated into five propositions:

(1) There has been, in the last twelve years, important, even basic, beneficial change in the lives of America's Negro population.

(2) This change has been produced primarily by a series of Supreme Court decisions (the 1954 School

Desegregation Decision, the 1957 Montgomery bus boy-
cott decision), and legislative enactments (the Civil
Rights Acts of 1957, 1960, 1964, 1965 and the Economic
Opportunity Acts).

(3) These decisions and enactments were made
possible by the pressure brought to bear on the various
branches of governments by a coalition of progressive
forces.

(4) The major elements of this coalition were, in
addition to Negroes, labor unions, liberals (academics,
writers, artists) and religious groups.

(5) This same coalition, expanded and strength-
ened, is the single agency that can muster the force to
produce the further governmental action necessary to
overcome the remaining obstacles to full Negro emancipation.

Black Power challenges the liberal coalition ideology on
every point:

(1) Basic changes have *not* been made in the lives
of the masses of America's Negroes.

(2) This lack of change is due to the fact that
the major pieces of litigation and legislation dealt with
problems in ways that affected only a tiny minority of
the Negro population, and what meaningful provisions
these laws do contain have gone virtually unenforced.

(3) The lack of enforcement is due to simple power
politics: the coalition has not had the "clout" to pass
tough legislation, or to get relatively powerful enactments enforced.

(4) The visible action and suffering of black people,
more than the friendly initiatives of sympathetic whites,
is the key to what power the coalition has had.

(5) In the face of its manifest failure to "deliver
the goods" of basic change for blacks, the liberal coalition is certainly open to major criticism; and in mapping
further strategy for the Negro liberation struggle it is
hardly irresponsible to suggest that coalitionism be re-
evaluated or even rejected.

Let us consider these assertions in detail.

Rustin himself points out that "it was the most mobility
conscious and relatively liberated groups in the Negro community — lower middle-class college students — who launched

the attack" on segregated public accommodations; and it has
largely been this highly "mobile" group, which constitutes a
very small segment of the Negro population, that has bene-
fitted from the movement's "victories." Further, he cites data
which, in his own words, show that *Negroes today are in worse
economic shape, live in worse slums, and attend more highly
segregated schools than in 1954.*"[33] Unemployment is up for
Negroes, the gulf between Negro and white incomes is greater,
unemployment for black youths is well over 30 percent. "To
put all this in the simplest and most concrete terms," Rustin
concludes, "the day-to-day lot of the ghetto Negro has not
been improved by the various judicial and legislative meas-
ures of the past decade."[34] This sentence, with a few pungent
adjectives inserted, could have been lifted straight from nearly
any of Stokely Carmichael's statements of the past several
months.

But Rustin does not seem to grasp the implications
of his admission. The primary implication is that the movement, for most Negroes, is more a rumor than a reality,
something that affects what they see on their television sets
but not what they see on their streets. Another significant
implication is that the weight given the movement's achievements is directly related to the class status of the group
evaluating it. To whites, whom the movement has made pain-
fully or angrily aware, not simply of Negro grievances but
just of Negro *existence,* the struggle's achievements seem
considerable (to liberals) or ominous (to conservatives);
to upper- and middle-class Negroes the struggle has removed
many barriers to full participation in the predominant patterns of consumption and mobility that their economic status
makes accessible to them. But to the mass of black men and
women in the ghettoes or the Black Belt, the impact of the
struggle is largely imperceptible. In the South, it has not
gotten rid of the racist sheriffs, it has not ended intimidation
by whites, it has not ended inferior and segregated education,
and it has not lifted Negroes from their economic deprivation and dependence on whites. In the North it has not
given blacks economic or political control of the suffocating

ghettoes, nor has it breached the invisible walls locking Negroes inside them. And the employment, housing and schools of Northern Negroes are in a state of deterioration, similar to that in the South, though for somewhat different reasons. In sum, Rustin's own citation of the facts are the best evidence for Black Power's first objection to coalitionism.

The Civil Rights Act of 1964[35] serves as a prime example of the movement's inability to affect the "nitty-gritty" of Negro existence, which could be called "failure by irrelevance." Let us consider this law, title by title, in terms of its impact on the lower-class Negro, North and South:

Title I. Dealing with voting requirements, this title makes it unlawful to apply different literacy requirements to persons of different races in federal elections; it also presumes anyone with a sixth-grade education to be literate. This title is irrelevant to the North, where voter registration is not the real source of the ghetto's political pathology. In the South it produced such political monstrosities as Alabama's last literacy test, which involved a form several pages long, references, vouchers, and over a hundred different test sheets. This was designed to "freeze" the electorate at its 1964 level (from which Negroes were virtually excluded) by making it so hard to register that *no one* could pass. Alabama's efforts, however, were largely wasted, because Title I was virtually unenforceable *and unenforced* anyway.

Title II. This contains the public accommodations section, against which the South and its Goldwaterite allies spent their fury in the ostensible defense of "Mrs. Murphy's" property rights. This title, again, is virtually irrelevant to the North. In the South, let me give as an example Selma, Alabama, where I worked for better than a year after the passage of this act.

No white restaurants complied with the Civil Rights Act until January of 1965, seven months after the act was passed. Then cadres of Negroes, organized by Dr. Martin Luther King's staff and accompanied by the watchful eyes of the national press, tested them. Many restaurants closed during the testing; those that complied with the least resistance were those who served a middle- and upper-class white clientele, and for whom an atmosphere of Southern tranquility was most important. After the testing campaign was over, most restaurants returned to ignoring or resisting the law; as late as June 1966 an integrated group was refused service at a pancake house on the main street. And as for lower-class places like the Silver Moon Cafe — in front of which Rev. James Reeb was fatally beaten and which is still the hangout for his killers — no one has even seriously suggested that their compliance be tested. Better than 80 percent of Selma's black majority is dirt-poor, and thus unlikely to be able to afford a meal any time soon at the Selma Del or the Holiday Inn, where they will be served. Title II is irrelevant to their lives, and Selma is not unusual.

This title also outlaws segregated restrooms at places like gasoline stations. Following its enactment, most "white" and "colored" signs came down from restroom doors. But they were soon replaced by unmbers: 1, 2, 3 and 4, or in smaller stations just 1, 2, and 3. The doors are, of course, locked "for the customer's protection" and the key must be obtained from an attendant. It should not be necessary to explain that different races get different keys.

Title III. This provides for the desegregation of public facilities — again largely irrelevant to the North. In the South it has resulted in the removal of "white" and "colored" signs from the dual sets of waiting rooms, water fountains, etc. in public buildings. Except in the largest cities, however, it has *not* eliminated the dual facilities. And in most places local citizens don't need signs to show them where to find "their" places.

Title IV. This authorizes the Attorney General to sue for desegregation of public educational institutions. It has a certain amount of potential effectiveness, but the fact is that better than 90 percent of the South's Negro students — and 65 percent nationwide — still attend segregated schools. This title is not necessarily irrelevant to the Negro's daily life, but so far it has been.

Title V. This title extends the life of the U.S. Civil

Rights Commission until 1968. The Commission is only an investigative body, having power to expose racism but none to deal with it.

Title VI. This is the heart of the law, apparently overlooked by most Southerners and Conservatives in their mad scramble to scuttle Title II. The title prohibits the use of federal funds for any project or program that practices discrimination.

This provision was responsible for most of the visible change in Selma before the Voting Rights Act. It, not Title III, brought down the "Colored Entrance" sign over the back door of the Dallas County Health Building. It "integrated" a summer Headstart Program. (The "integration" amounted to the hiring of one *white* teacher, a seminary student who spent a summer working in the movement. This came only after much pressure was applied by the Office of Economic Opportunity. All the other teachers and students were *black,* because the program had to be open to all if it was to get funds; and so no whites would have anything to do with it, except for the school board that controlled the funds.) Title VI also placed two dozen or so black faces in white elementary schools. And for awhile it held forth the possibility of control of the county anti-poverty program by organized poor (i.e., black people).

From these beginnings, all based on Title VI, one could draw hope if the government had continued to push the gains; but it has not. As the South began to develop sophisticated methods of evading the law, a skittish Congress cut the already miniscule enforcement funds without which the law is a dead letter. Thus Southern blacks are likely to be stuck indefinitely with a spotty, meaningless tokenism (Title VI has yet to touch the Selma hospitals, for example), while surrounded by vast areas of open defiance of the law coupled with quiet efforts to retrench the present system behind a better public relations mask. In the North, Title VI has yet to be used effectively against obvious patterns of *de facto* segregation in our large cities, as we shall see in more detail a little later. This big gun of the Civil Rights Act has so far fired little but ceremonial volleys.

Title VII. This title embodies the Equal Employment section, another potential force for significant action. But enforcement is so cumbersome and drawn out that even determined efforts to make use of it could and would take years to effect significant changes. Moreover, the Negro's experience even with voluntary "equal employment opportunity" has been that when jobs *are* opened to all who are "qualified," the result, because of the inferiority of Negro education, is at best only token black representation. Equal employment opportunity employers are continually, so we are told, "seeking" but "unable" to find "qualified" Negroes for their open jobs; as someone has said, the Negro Ph.D. today has it made. But before they have to face employers, the mass of American blacks are rendered by other institutions incapable of competing with white workers. The doors opened by this title will be those through which few Negroes can pass without special assistance. We saw (p. 15) how the Commission created to administer this section is limping along with only three of five Commissioners and a backlog of 81,500 cases, a portent which suggests that this title is little more effective than Title I.

Title VIII. This directs the Secretary of Commerce to take a survey of voter-registration in areas selected by the Civil Rights Commission.

Title IX. The Attorney General is authorized by this title to intervene in certain legal proceedings involving the Fourteenth Amendment. It is not a significant weapon.

Title X. This title creates the Community Relations Service, an interesting vestigial organ in the federal civil rights corpus. Understaffed and underfinanced, like the rest of the national machinery, the service is supposed to work behind the scenes to secure voluntary compliance with civil rights statutes. This approach has some potential relevance in situations where essentially marginal issues are at stake. But the Service has no conceivable relevance to the basic problems of black Americans, North or South, and well deserves the obscurity it has enjoyed.

Title XI. This last Title covers a miscellaneous group of provisions. It contains nothing important.

And that's it. The un- or under- employed, semi-literate slum or black-belt dweller — who forms the majority of blacks — find little comfort in the provisions of the Civil Rights Act of 1964, and still less in their enforcement. Little has changed for him because of it, and not much more is likely to. Similar criticisms can be directed toward the other major pieces of legislation concerned with civil rights. The Voting Rights Act of 1965 is a fairly tough bill that has been enforced only enough to make headlines, not enough really to change the political life of the South. It is irrelevant to the North. The Economic Opportunity Act of 1964 is a bill with some good ideas, but it was appropriated only about 6 percent of the money needed if the Act was to have real impact on poverty. The Office of Economic Opportunity it created is now losing all its weapons to Congressional counterattacks and a *real* war in Vietnam. The failures, through irrelevance and nonenforcement, of federal attempts to meet the needs of American Negroes are clear, when the facts are examined.[36] Black Power's critique of them is, unfortunately, virtually unassailable.

The laws we have examined were in fact passed as a result of pressure mobilized by the liberal coalition, and are evidence of the coalition's power. By now, however, it should be clear that this evidence is rather ambiguous. Why, we feel constrained to ask, has the coalition's power not resulted in tougher legislation or better enforcement? Does the coalition indeed *have* the power to force action on the black man's needs for jobs, housing, schools, and protection? Bayard Rustin is confident that the coalition does.

> We [the liberals] are responsible for the growth of the "black power" concept because we have not used our own power to insure the full implementation of the bills whose passage we were strong enough to win, and we have not

mounted the necessary campaign for winning a decent minimum wage and extended benefits.[37]

Black Power adherents doubt whether the coalition is powerful enough to fulfill either objective. There are many cases that support such doubts, but two examples will suffice for our purposes. First is the case of Chicago's school money, and second the battle over the Child Development Group of Mississippi. Both involved the implementation of federal programs, one in the North and one in the South. Both offered direct challenges to the power of the liberal coalition to insure implementation. And both cases took the measure of liberal coalition power.

Everyone knows that Chicago's schools are segregated.[38] Here as elsewhere in the North it was not necessary to enshrine segregation in local statutes; the job was done much more quietly — as is Northern custom — and nearly as effectively, through the institution known as the "neighborhood school." If a neighborhood is lily white, then naturally its neighborhood school is lily-white, and vice versa for Negro neighborhoods. U.S. Commissioner of Education Francis Keppel, who perhaps knew law better than he knew politics, declared in early October of 1965 that the racial condition of Chicago's school system was in flagrant violation of Title VI of the Civil Rights Act of 1964, and he ordered $30 million worth of federal aid money withheld from the system.

But everyone knew, with the possible exception of Mr. Keppel, that Richard J. Daley, the Democratic Mayor of the Windy City, is czar of the most potent city machine in the nation. Mr. Keppel soon found this out. Immediately after the announcement, Congressman Roman C. Pucinski, a loyal Daley mouthpiece, began declaiming furiously to the nation's press about states rights and federal arrogation of authority. Republican Senator from Illinois Everett Dirksen also raised his mellifluous voice in concern. Shortly thereafter Mayor Daley made a trip to New York City, where the President of the United States was welcoming Pope Paul VI to our shores. The President and the Mayor conferred briefly, and Daley returned home. Within hours, Chicago had its $30 million,

Mr. Keppel — we may venture to guess — had a headache, and the South had learned a lesson it has not forgotten.

We have heard no more from the Office of Education about Title VI and Northern city schools. Commissioner Keppel has departed the office for other pursuits. Perhaps he acted out of naivete; perhaps not. Perhaps he wanted to see just how far Title VI would be supported when it began to affect some of the political beneficiaries of the present system. Certainly he forced the Daley juggernaut to show its muscle in public, and to make clear to all who had eyes to see just how deeply enmeshed the Administration is with the forces supporting racism. And where were the liberals? But Daley *is* a liberal; he *supported* the same Civil Rights Act that he thus eviscerated.

Let us compare what happened in Chicago with the 1966 battle over the Child Development Group of Mississippi, an encounter in which the liberal coalition came out swinging and in full force.[39]

The Child Development Group of Mississippi (CDGM) is a statewide network of Operation Headstart Centers operated mostly by poor Negroes. Many of its staff are veterans of the civil rights movement. This is the first real experience most of them have had of controlling any institution. CDGM is widely known as the best Headstart program in the nation, the one most true to the Economic Opportunity Act's language about "maximum feasible participation of the poor."

Such success, and the things Mississippi Negroes are learning from it, is of course very threatening to a Deep South status quo that needs Negroes who are without resources, semi-literate and, most of all, totally dependent on whites. Consequently, CDGM has had a stormy history, and in 1965 barely weathered a determined attack by the Magnolia State's Senator John Stennis.

In the fall of 1966, when CDGM applied for funds for another year's operation, opposition again arose. Re-funding the program, most observers concluded, was a risk that poverty chief Sargent Shriver was not prepared to take. After an especially long hot summer racially, with the real war in Vietnam escalated and the "backlash" riding the hustings, the Office of Economic Opportunity was very much on the defensive and eager to avoid controversy. In early October, Shriver announced that he was not giving CDGM any more money, and was funding instead a substitute group that was loyalist-Democrat dominated and very likely to be much concerned about the "qualifications" of its workers.[40]

As soon as news of Shriver's decision hit the papers, the liberal coalition rushed to CDGM's rescue. The Citizen's Crusade Against Poverty, an offspring of Walter Reuther's United Auto Workers, spearheaded the effort. Martin Luther King called on Mr. Shriver about the matter. Liberals in both houses of Congress made their feelings known to OEO. The Americans for Democratic Action endorsed CDGM. The National Council of Churches joined in. A committee was formed which inserted a large advertisement, "Say It Isn't So, Sargent Shriver," in *The New York Times*.[41] The whole force of the liberal coalition was mobilized behind the resuscitation of CDGM. Finally, near the end of December, Shriver yielded and CDGM got its money. The liberal coalition had won.

In this encounter the roles were somewhat similar to those in the shorter Chicago drama, but with the players reversed: this time the liberals were trying to repeat Mayor Daley's feat and force the villain Shriver (and CDGM's Congressional enemies) to release the funds. The liberals' performance in this role is instructive. First of all, the money in question — about $8 million — was less than a third of the Chicago stakes. The Office of Economic Opportunity is, moreover, a much less weighty government agency than the Office of Education. Yet it still took the liberal coalition, with all flags unfurled, all stops out, and all its alleged power unleashed, almost three months to pry the cash out of OEO, whereas Daley had done the job on over three times as much, from a tougher outfit, in little more than three days.

The coalition won the CDGM battle, it is true; but the circumstances of the victory strongly suggest that the liberals' political batters are not even in the same league with the likes of Daley. Let us remember that CDGM, valuable as it unquestionably is, is still only peripheral to real solutions to the problems and needs of Mississippi's half-million black people. And if such a victory cost the liberal coalition three months of all-out, exhausting effort, what are we to expect from it in a battle for enactment or enforcement of legislation which *can* speak meaningfully to the Negro's basic needs — especially when any such program (such as Title VI) almost inevitably will bring the coalition into conflict with people like Mayor Daley in the North as well as Stennis in the South?

These are two of the more widely known challenges to liberal coalition power since the passage of the Civil Rights and Economic Opportunity Acts. In Chicago, liberals were caught unawares by Commissioner Keppel's action and totally bypassed by Daley's swift counter-thrust; once liberals had their wits about them, they did little but futilely denounce the Administration retreat — virtually admitting that they could do nothing about it. The CDGM mess resembled Chicago, but with the roles reversed; but they couldn't match the Mayor's feat. Observers, including Chicago and Mississippi Negroes, whose schools and children were affected, cannot but repeat the questions we began with: Why couldn't the liberal coalition bail out Commissioner Keppel as well as CDGM? Or press effectively for the tough enforcement of decent laws that is so lacking? Where, indeed, *is* the liberals' power?

EXAMINATION OF THE ELEMENTS OF THE COALITION

Black Power advocates suggest that liberals have a view of their own importance that is exaggerated and not justifiable in terms of the power realities in this country. More specifically, Black Power feels that the coalition as it is presently constituted does *not* have enough "clout" to produce a real governmental attack on the basic problems of the mass of Negroes. An examination of the elements of the coalition — which Rustin defines as being labor, liberals, and churches —

may help us understand this allegation. Let us begin with labor.

James A. Wechsler, a coalitionist critic of Black Power, has written with dismay of the ills afflicting labor today, especially in regard to matters of "liberal" concern:

> There is little residue of feeling that organized labor is seriously engaged in battles for justice; only rarely — as in the California Agricultural Workers struggle — does the AFL-CIO seem genuinely concerned with the fate of those who have not already achieved the dividends of unionism.[42]

David Danzig, writing in *Commentary,* has also spoken of labor's actual commitment to the elimination of poverty and racism:

> One might expect organized labor to begin to concern itself with the economic needs of this second America. But for the most part the unions in practice act as a conservative establishment that is mainly worried about maintaining its prerogatives against the sweeping changes of automation.[43]

This conservatism has definite racial elements. Kenneth Clark, in his excellent book *Dark Ghetto,* has dealt at length with the relationship between blacks and the unions:

> The [American] white worker has felt much less a proletariat psychologically than his counterpart in Europe because of the existence of a black proletariat in subjugated status beneath him.... Whites will have to risk their own status if Negroes are to be admitted into the world of work as peers, and the white worker has understood this instinctively. ... When the Negro starts moving he threatens almost total collapse of white status and of the white worker's world. This is a matter of bread and butter and self-respect to the white worker.... He has no time for a stereotype liberal response in behalf of civil rights.[44]

Certainly this description fits the attitude showing through the remarks of a white priest in a working-class Chicago neighborhood where open-housing marchers were greeted with naked savagery last summer:

> "These are good people ... Policemen and schoolteachers and workingmen. Put yourself in their place. You've given 20 years to building up your property — you're in a nice

neighborhood now, you have a little house worth fifteen or twenty thousand dollars maybe. Some colored moves into your block, and your property drops down two, three thousand dollars."

"That doesn't have to happen" [protested the interviewer]. "Everybody doesn't have to sell and run."

"You know what those real estate people do."

"But you don't have to let them bust the block. You can decide to stay. The church could even help to educate your parishioners."

"What am I supposed to say to a man when he's worked for 20 years and keeps up his house and his property, and one of the colored moves into the block? Now you know how they live — pretty soon their friends move in and there are six or seven families living in the house."[45]

Pete, a white resident of the Chicago suburb of Cicero, makes the attitudes even more plain:

"Look, you have to know these people," Pete says. "The most important thing in the world to them is their home. It's maybe a crummy little house just like the house next door, but they busted their ass for 20 years to get that house, and they paint it and they take care of it and mow the lawn, and they live good in Cicero. Nobody bothers nobody. They like it the way it is, and they don't want any Negro — I mean nigger — to move in and louse it up."[46]

Dr. Clark also discusses the labor movement's treatment of Negroes, with a frankness that must grate on the liberal ear:

Racism has been one of the persistently debilitating facts in the American labor movement. . . . In the highest levels of labor unions, the status of Negroes is almost invisible. In New York City no Negro holds a position of primary power in organized labor. Negroes have been effectively segregated in American labor, much as in American churches, with their "own" unions such as the railroad brotherhood of Sleeping Car Porters. . . . Where Negroes are singled out as labor representatives, they hold these posts at the pleasure of white leadership. Even in unions where most workers are Negro or Puerto Rican, the actual top leadership is predominantly white and often seems responsive more to the wishes of management than to the people they allegedly serve.[47]

Clark cites the International Ladies Garment Workers Union as an example of his thesis. Investigators for the NAACP uncovered the existence of segregated sub-units within the ILGWU locals in the Empire City, and virtual non-representation of nonwhites (Negroes and Puerto Ricans) in the union's hierarchy. The union, which dominates New York's garment industry and is the mainstay of the state's Liberal Party, did not dispute the charges.[48] Many of the building trades and craft unions have become preserves for various groups that have shown themselves viciously determined to retain their lily white, ingrown character.

Whitney Young, whose statistics-minded Urban League is in a position to know such things, also wrote revealingly of labor's actual treatment of Negro workers in its own baili-wick:

> ... In the upper reaches, at the parent, or international union level, discrimination has been largely erased from the books.
>
> But at the local affiliate level, exclusion is practiced all too successfully. And at the rank-and-file level, the AFL-CIO and the international unions themselves have great difficulty in bringing about change. In fact, it is because they lack leverage that George Meany testified before Congressional committees in favor of federal fair employment legislation with sanctions against offending unions as well as employers. However, the history of union bias in states with fair employment laws and commissions and the fact that the National Labor Relations Board and federal labor laws have made no headway against local union discrimination are discouraging.[49]

Equally discouraging is the performance of the federal Equal Employment Opportunity Commission, whose performance we have referred to earlier (p. 66). *The Nation,* editorially surveying this Commission's record, observed that "the history of the commission so far offers little hope that [its] objectives will be achieved."[50] We must agree with Silberman's comment about this situation:

> Much of the Negro cynicism about white liberals stems from their discovery that all too many ardent advocates of integration turn out to be for integration only in someone

else's neighborhood or someone else's school district or someone else's trade union.[51]

We can see from this a little more about the character
of the labor movement. In Bayard Rustin's words, "Despite
its obvious faults, it has been the largest single organized
force in this country pushing for progressive social legislation."[52] But the most "obvious" of labor's faults is that its
efforts have always been for the benefit of its membership.
There is surely nothing wrong with this, but when much of
this membership sees Negro job and housing advancement as
a threat to its own position, and when labor's own backyard
is scheduled to become a major battleground for the Negro's
struggle, the labor movement's continuing contribution and
dedication to a coalition working in the Negro's interest must
be viewed with skepticism and trepidation.

James Wechsler may be cited again, for he has outlined
some of the internal regeneration labor must seek if it is
to offer much to such a coalition:

> I have argued [see above, pp. 44f.] that the future of the
> civil rights cause hinged on the evolution of a strategy of
> coalition as urged by Philip Randolph, Bayard Rustin, and
> others. In many respects the same test confronts labor; only
> in a new, large alliance with the multitudes of those most
> oppressed can it hope to regain its soul. But such a prospect
> would require perhaps implausible revolutions in attitudes.
> It would risk the alienation of some new "aristocrats of labor"
> who have found their way to lily-white suburbias. It would
> mean a vast, crusading educational effort among unionists
> susceptible to old bigotries. It would entail a large altera-
> tion in approach to the unorganized consumer who views
> himself as the victim of a management-labor squeeze.[53]

Mr. Wechsler does not appear confident about the likelihood
of such "implausible revolutions" inside Big Labor. Even if
such efforts were begun now, they would take years to show
results. They remain at this point but a gleam in Mr. Wechsler's eye, and the distance from there to reality is, unfortunately, considerably further.

Labor at least has its own constituency; but most liberal
intellectuals depend for support on institutions: universities,

corporations, ad agencies, etc., which in most cases they do not control. C. Wright Mills has summed up the meaning of this situation:

> Between the intellectual and his potential public stand technical, economic and social structures which are owned and operated by others. The medium of pamphlets offered to Tom Paine a direct channel to readers that in the world of mass-advertising-supported publications clearly cannot be afforded by the dissenter. If the intellectual becomes the hired man of an information industry, his general aims must, of course, be set by the decisions of others rather than by his own integrity.[54]

Hans J. Morgenthau, presently Senior Research Fellow for the Council on Foreign Relations, has analyzed the state of contemporary intellectuals *vis a vis* especially the government:

> Reflecting ... upon the relations that exist at present between the intellectual of America and the government of the United States, one cannot escape, however much one would like to, two conclusions: the administration has tried to discredit, silence and corrupt [them], and it has in good measure succeeded with the support of the intellectuals themselves.
>
> ... Large segments of the intellectual world have been silenced or corrupted. This is especially true of those segments which are professionally concerned with the activities of government. If one examines, for instance, the lists of intellectuals who have gone on record against the war in Vietnam, one is struck by the relative paucity of political scientists. One is also struck by the frequency with which those who remain silent in public express their opposition in private.
>
> ... The government does not leave the silence and subservience of the intellectuals to chance. It has at its disposal a plethora of varied, subtle and insidious instruments with which to forge reliable ties with large segments of the intellectual world. ... These ties are both formal and informal, and the latter are the more dangerous to intellectual freedom as they consist of the intellectuals' unconscious adaptation to imperceptible social and political pressures.
>
> The intimate connection which research contracts have established between the government and the universities has recently been brought to public attention. It stands to reason

that an academic who is working on such a contract or who expects to work on one is not likely to question the basic policies of the government, either within his contractual research or outside it. Thus the interests and expectations of the government not only determine the subject matter of contractual research but also influence ever so subtly its scope and in a certain measure its results.

Aside from these formal contractual relations with which the government is able to keep large segments of the academic community silent or render them subservient, the government disposes of a whole gamut of professional and social rewards serving the same purpose. . . . By adroitly promising, dispensing and withholding them, it keeps a large segment of the academic community at bay. The academic, by accepting one or the other of these rewards, enters into a subtle and insidious relationship with the government which imperceptibly transforms his position of independent judge to that of client and partisan.[55]

The majority of the funds spent in academic research comes from the government.[56] Much of the rest comes from private corporations. Most research is handled on a contract basis, directly between the academician who is to do the research and the agency or company who wants it done. The dependence, then, of most of the academic community which is engaged in research is assured, and their silence almost certain.

Bayard Rustin has characterized the militant Negro attitude toward intellectuals thus:

It has become fashionable in some no-win Negro circles to decry the white liberals as the main enemy (his hypocrisy is what sustains racism); by virtue of this reverse recitation of the reactionary's litany (liberalism leads to socialism, which leads to Communism) the Negro is left in majestic isolation, except for a tiny band of fervent white initiates.[57]

But here Rustin has grossly exaggerated the Black Power attitude toward liberals, especially toward corporate-academic liberals. Most such liberals work within large institutions, expending their energies on objectives defined by someone else. They are, by and large, true Organization Men, willing employees who are well paid for their services. SNCC has rejected such liberals, not because they are in any sense "the main enemy," but simply because they are mostly dead weight. They do not control their employers' policies, which in most cases are solidly enmeshed in the status quo, and consequently realistic Black Power strategists do not even take them much into account. We will discuss the implications of Rustin's statement and the reaction it represents later (Chapter 4); here it will suffice to suggest that much of the liberals' hue and cry over their rejection by the militants can be seen as a defense mechanism against the intimation that they are not indeed important enough to be taken into account in the militants' plans.

Churches, the third major element in the grand coalition, present a picture similar in many respects to that of the academic-corporate liberals. Most major denominational structures are large, bureaucratic, corporate-style institutions, with much the same organizational ethos as their secular counterparts. Predictably, most church-based liberalism is similarly without any actual institutional control. In addition, most ministers are answerable to congregations and their attitudes. A situation that is paradigmatic of what effects these factors can have was recently described in *Trans-ACTION*,[58] a social science journal. While in training at the Urban Training Center for Christian Missions in Chicago in June of 1965, 47 ministers, from 17 states and 7 denominations, were urged to join a march protesting the city's *de facto* segregated schools. Forty marched in the first demonstration; but three days and several hundred arrests later, only 24 showed up for a march that they were sure would (and did) end in their being arrested. The attrition was found to correlate very closely to (1) the vigor with which a minister's denomination had endorsed civil rights, and (2) the minister's estimate of his congregation's attitude toward his continuing involvement in such protests. The article interpreted the data thus:

> The ministers who participate in civil rights demonstrations ... add up to only a comparative handful. The vast majority of ministers, who may support the civil rights movement from their pulpits, repeatedly balk at active involvement.

> Did the minister's denominations have anything to do
> with the extent of their participation in the protests? We
> found that it definitely did. . . . The simple dichotomy be-
> tween strong and moderate denominational commitment was
> directly related to the involvement pattern of the trainees.
>
> An even more important determinant, we found, was
> the specific congregation's attitude on the civil rights ques-
> tion: the UTC trainees tended to act in a way they perceived
> would be acceptable to their parishioners back home.[59]

One-quarter of the trainees were pastors in white suburban
churches. Only 60 percent of this sub-group marched at all,
and but one was arrested. The less sympathetic the denomination or congregation, the less active the minister is likely
to be.

Another important factor influencing participation is
the proximity of the protest to the minister's hometown. This
is not an isolated phenomenon:

> The local parish ministry of Chicago did not appear to
> be widely represented in the 1965 summer marches. . . . This
> impression of Chicago's situation is consistent with observa-
> tions of civil rights activity in other areas.[60]

The attitude of liberal clerics was provocatively outlined
in *The Christian Century* in a report on a massive ecumeni-
cal convocation during the push for passage of the Civil
Rights Act of 1964:

> Four thousand clerical and lay leaders of the Protestant,
> Roman Catholic, and Jewish faiths, meeting together in Wash-
> ington's McDonough Memorial Gymnasium at Georgetown
> University on April 28, called for an immediate passage of
> the civil rights bill to end the nation's *moral crisis*.[61]

The clerics identified the civil rights bill with the effects that
visible American racism had on their consciences. When the
law was passed, we must presume that their "moral crisis"
was resolved and their consciences calmed; in any case, much
religious agitation for civil rights dissipated. But racism had
not, in fact, been vanquished; it had barely lost a skirmish.
The whole stance of organized religious support for civil
rights, as exemplified in the Washington convocation, suggests

that it is aimed more at salving white consciences than in solving black people's problems.

There are some few insurgents in most denominations, generally clergymen not tied to congregations, who seem profoundly and creatively dedicated to a theologically based radicalism. But if one may generalize from the Chicago trainees' reactions, the liberal church support for a grand coalition can be expected to falter as the coalition's objectives begin to affect such bases of its support as white suburbs (with their "neighborhood churches" as well as their "neighborhood schools"), white jobs and white political machines with which various urban hierarchies are intertwined. Such areas, of course, are just where the struggle is likely to be in the future.

To conclude, let us recall Bayard Rustin's charges that Black Power "diverts the movement from a meaningful debate over strategy and tactics...."[62] It seems evident to me that he considers debate meaningful only if it takes place in the context of coalitionism. But Black Power's questioning of the coalition's strength and potential seems to me not only appropriate and well founded but *imperative* if we are to be realistic about the future of the movement. Thus the charge seems beside the point.

Rustin also believes that Black Power "isolates the Negro community."[63] The best response I have heard to this objection was made by Mrs. Mattie Humphrey, a Philadelphia (Pa.) Black Power worker, in reply to a question about the racial "polarization" Black Power allegedly induces:

> "Polarization? We don't worry about polarization of the races, because in this country the races have been polarized from the beginning — it's only some whites who don't know it, and now they're beginning to find out."[64]

As long as America's blacks remain in a condition of powerlessness, poverty, and self-contempt because of nationwide patterns of institutionalized racism, this polarization will remain. Coalitionist victories have yet to touch the sources of this polarization. The shift of the movement's battlegrounds to the Northern liberals' own backyards is far more responsible for what the whites are now calling "polarization" than is any slogan of black people; it is this shift which has made it impossible to conceal any longer the polarization that was always there. Rustin should be, but isn't, looking elsewhere for the sources of this "isolation" he refers to.

Finally, Rustin contends that Black Power "encourages the growth of anti-Negro forces," growth exemplified by the backlash. Carmichael answered this with the example of Cicero and its response to a Negro march for open-housing: "What you saw in Cicero was simply a system of white supremacy defending itself when it is threatened. There was no 'backlash'; there was nothing to lash back *from*."[65]

This is the theme of our analysis of the liberal coalition: to demand an end to black powerlessness both *North and South,* is to reveal the coalition's numerous Achilles heels, and make visible the actual extent of its interdependence with the roots of racism. Rustin himself says of liberals disenchanted with the Negro movement because of Black Power's appearance that they "leave us no choice but to question their original motivation."[66] More important, he does not question the motives of those who *stay.* If there is anything Black Power has accomplished, it is the unmasking of many so-called "friends" of the Negro, for the well-disguised racists that they really were.

The militants of SNCC and CORE define power as the capacity to "speak to the needs" of the mass of people. By this definition, the liberal coalition recommended by Rustin either has little effective power, or, if it does have any, it has yet to exercise it in a meaningful way. Moreover, blacks can hardly help but perceive that the coalition's major "victories" (the Civil Rights Acts of 1964 and 1965) rode the waves of public indignation that followed upon official brutality inflicted upon Negroes marching unarmed in public streets before the world's press media. This effect was heightened when the violence also affected sympathetic whites (Rev. James Reeb, Mrs. Viola Liuzzo; but who remembers Jimmie Lee Jackson?). Negroes are right to question whether the coalition can win anything on its own initiative (without bleeding Negroes and whites) or on its own territory (e.g., Chicago). They are right to demand a re-evaluation of the whole basis and objectives of coalitionism. And liberal whites must, if they are honest, begin to take a long, hard look at the meaning and the potential of their "liberalism."

Chapter Three
LIBERALS AND BLACK POWER

Black Power is very skeptical about the existing civil rights coalition. But it is clear from the statements of its advocates that, contrary to the charges of Rustin, *et al.*, they have not and do not reject the *idea* of coalition. Lincoln Lynch, Associate Director of CORE, told an interviewer: "We will work with anybody, literally anybody, to achieve equality of opportunity, dignity of the individual, and power in the communities of Black America."[1] It is normal journalistic practice to interpret such declarations as heralding an amalgamation with the Black Muslims, Negro gun clubs, or other such "extreme" or "subversive" elements. I would like to suggest, however, that Mr. Lynch's sweeping remarks mean that CORE would be willing to work even with *whites* who could bring real resources to their struggle. We have heard Stokely Carmichael voice similar sentiments:

> When the black community is able to ... negotiate with other groups from a position of organized strength, the possibilities of meaningful political alliances on specific issues will be increased. That is a rule of politics; and there is no reason why it should not operate here.[2]

He told *Jet* magazine and its Negro readership: "We are not opposed to whites helping in this struggle. But they must understand that Negroes must lead. We are working to develop black power independent of white power. As I say, we will work with whites."[3] In SNCC's newspaper *The Movement,* Carmichael stated over a year ago:

> No, I don't reject coalitions; what I say is that Negroes have to realize that when you form coalitions you aim toward what people call "national interest," and national interest is never the same as Negro interest. So they have to maintain their own interest first, then certainly they can form other coalitions.[4]

So the question is not one of exclusion because of color, or a determination by Negroes to "go it alone," but rather a hardheaded insistence that coalitions will be evaluated on the basis of what *power* (still defined as the capacity to "speak to the needs" of blacks) erstwhile allies of any shade can offer the movement. Liberal whites who still wish a role in the black struggle must ask themselves what meaningful resources they now have or are likely to have to offer organized black people.

BLACK POWER STRATEGY

Black Power strategy, the plan in terms of which coalitions are to be evaluated, calls for the development of institutions — political and economic, especially the latter — which blacks can control and which can meet the Negro's physical needs and his needs for cultural self-preservation. This is not what critics have labeled it, "separatism," any more than such institutions as the Negro-owned North Carolina Mutual Life Insurance Company or the Jewish-owned Hebrew National Food Stores are "separatist" organizations. This demand merely expresses certain assumptions about power that should be obvious but which seem to be very difficult for many liberals to grasp and keep hold of: namely, that to gain a measure of power, for change or just for self-preservation in American society, an individual or group must either *take over* existing institutions (as certain immigrant groups took over some city political structures) or *develop institutions of its own* (as did other groups through labor unions). These institutions must be able to do at least three things: (1) give the group some control over its life, (2) support the individual or group economically, and (3) confront other institutions on an equal footing.

Such institutions are the necessary precondition, the

real basis on which "meaningful political alliances" can be built; without such an institutional base, all an individual or group can do is, in essence, *beg* for what are really handouts from groups which *do* have such institutional resources and power. The traditional stance of most civil rights groups has amounted to such supplication. For example, take this description of Urban League strategy for an international trip with Henry Ford II, Roger Blough of U.S. Steel, and other business leaders, recounted by League Executive Director Whitney Young, who was to travel with the group:

> In the casual give and take of a trip like this I'll be able to say some things to these men. . . .
> Take the matter of housing: "You ought to be in favor of this bill," I'll tell them. You build offices and plants in American cities and the Negro poor are taking over the cities. They're not taxpayers, they're tax consumers. You pay the taxes. How can you bow to a few real-estate men and builders?
> It's not a question of morality, it's a question of economics. It's an investment. Measure the cost of urban slums, the cost of crime, the police protection, the welfare, the lack of productivity. Compared to that, the money that can be spent rehabilitating these slums is a valuable investment. It may look costly at first, but the "domestic Marshall plan" I proposed years ago will be cheaper in the long run.[5]

An influential Negro college president, speaking in the same columns as did Young, was more candid about the process:

> We have to know how to handle the white man. A lot of Southern white men are pretty dumb, but if you handle them the right way, they'll do the right thing. The important thing is to make sure they get all the credit, so they can say, "look at what we've done for you."[6]

No Negro, I think, could read these statements without seeing their resemblance to the accommodating spirit of Booker T. Washington. Young's position, despite its mask of statistics and "good business sense," is still that of the suppliant, wheedling and cajoling favors from the powerful for the powerless. Young's trip is over, and as yet neither Ford nor U. S. Steel have made public any desire to support any of the programs Young is pushing. But shortly after the trip the Urban League received a $400,000 grant from the Ford Foundation, along with a promise for more in the future. Young got a letter from Henry Ford II ("You are a great guy and run a wonderful organization") containing a check for $100,000. Young considers the trip a success.[6a]

I don't understand how Negroes can be proud of "leaders" who publicly admit that such pleading is their best hope. Yet Young and his Urban League are extolled by both liberal whites and blacks as the real powerhouses of Negro advancement. Carl Rowan admiringly but revealingly summed up the accomplishments of the Urban League's approach:

> Young had been so shrewd at making whites feel guilty about the Negro's plight and worried about the future that the foundations and big corporations had pumped more than $2.8 million into the 1966 Urban League budget, as against $300,000 in 1961.[7]

Unquestionably, then, Young has sold the Urban League well. But not everyone regards this sort of salesmanship with equal approbation. James Booker, a columnist for Harlem's moderate weekly *The Amsterdam News,* wrote somewhat sardonically of Young's junketing:

> The Urban League's Whitney Young, Jr. is off on an Eastern European tour sponsored by a major magazine while Urban League affiliates are getting more and more foundation and antipoverty funds. The A. Philip Randolph Institute, with Bayard Rustin at the helm, got a big chunk from George Meany and is hoping to get more from Walter Reuther. Will the real Negro organization, supported by "Negro green power," please stand up?[8]

There is good reason for Booker's skepticism, which reduces to the old saw about the man who pays the piper calling the tune, a theme we have heard before when we looked at academic, corporate, and church liberals. In addition, despite Rowan's adulation, a detached observer would have to say that the League's budget increase from 1961 to 1966 in relation to the amounts of money needed to make serious inroads on Negro poverty and its effects, is but an increase of from one drop in the bucket to two or three. At that rate it will take decades of such salesmanship for the League to show any results among the masses of blacks. We can also detect in this strategy the implicit acceptance of integration-by-assimilation, with the pitch being that Young's plans are really just a good investment, which of course is going to pay off big for Ford and U. S. Steel (remember General Motors and Bank of America?). We already know what the militants think of this (see pp. 18ff.).

The SNCC-CORE call for a black-controlled economic base is nothing new. Marcus Garvey's Universal Negro Improvement Association launched many ambitious black-owned business ventures, such as the Black Star Steamship Line. Their failure was due more to internal mismanagement and chicanery than to any inherent defect in the idea.[9] The Black Muslim's newspaper each week is dotted with "help wanted" ads for the Nation of Islam's flourishing stores and other enterprises. Elijah Muhammad's economic program may yet become a major force in the ghetto's economy.

In any case, if Carmichael and other black militants are serious about giving the Negro's pride in his culture a permanent foundation, they have no alternative but to seek the development of a black economic base which is responsive to the black community. The reason for this was stated clearly by a Negro field hand in Lowndes County, Alabama, who was among the hundreds brought by white plantation owners who were also their employers and landlords, to register after the Voting Rights Act was passed. A SNCC worker approached the field hand and asked him if he was going to let his boss man tell him how to vote. "Thass right," the field hand replied; "and if *you* give me a place to live and some land to work, *you* can tell me how to vote."[10] The sharecropper had a point; it was just such black votes that defeated the Lowndes County Freedom Party at the polls in November 1966.

Mr. John Hulett, the Party Chairman, afterward reflected soberly on the election's meaning:

> We were foolish to think those Negroes on the planta-
> tion would vote for us. They're scared. Scared they'll get
> kicked off the land.
> We've got to provide for them the bare minimum in
> security if they get hurt supporting us.[11]

The Party's candidate for sheriff, Sidney Logan, Jr., added:

> We need some kind of finances to help people stay in
> the County when they get kicked off the land. White people
> got so much land and got so many tenants on it, the boss man
> always goin' to control those votes and the elections.[12]

The Lowndes County Freedom Party is turning its attention to the development of an independent economic base
as the prerequisite for effective exercise of its potential
political strength in the county. The difference between
Lowndes County and Harlem is only one of degree. Kenneth
Clark has shown clearly how the economy of Harlem is
owned by whites who suck the community's meager resources away into outside coffers[13]; other ghettoes are not
much different. Too many ghetto Negroes employed by whites
— like their Southern brethren — can be expected to vote with
their stomachs against their pride when the two conflict; and
no one can reasonably blame them for doing so.

It is important to note that Carmichael's calls for independent economic enterprises have always been in terms
of cooperatives, businesses owned by their consumer or pro-
ducer members rather than by private entrepreneurs. There
were Negro slave owners before Emancipation, and there are
Negro slumlords today who bilk poverty-stricken blacks as
remorselessly as any white renter for the privilege of living in
rat-infested tenements. So obviously it is not enough just to
replace indifferent absentee *white* ownership with indifferent
absentee *black* ownership. Black Power urges Negroes to
organize, build and cooperatively run their own apartment
houses, stores, banks, and factories, etc., so these institutions
can truly reflect the needs and desires of their member-
owners.[14]

Cooperative businesses include most types of enterprises.
They operate on a nonprofit basis, returning surpluses to their

membership in proportion to a member's patronage (in contrast to a stock corporation's profit dividends to stockholders who may never patronize the business). Boards of directors are elected on a one member one vote basis (instead of the stock corporation's one *share* one vote).[15] Cooperatives have a long and distinguished history in the United States, and are regularly endorsed as shining examples of patriotic Americanism in action by every major political leader from the President down.[16] Carmichael's call for cooperatives in the ghetto could therefore hardly be considered "radical" or "subversive," though if they were successful they would no doubt cut into some white businessmen's favorite markets. Moreover, such enterprises could provide the base of support for a Negro politics that is truly responsible to the Negro community at large, and make it possible at last for blacks to vote for both their dignity and their stomachs on the same ticket. It is not a complicated program, and I find it practical and persuasive.

BLACK POWER AND WHITE POWER

Earlier we alluded to the fact (p. 78) that Negro militants regard their liberal white "allies" as having, at least up to now, little relevance to the power realities they are attempting to deal with. What hostility the militants have directed toward these white friends is mostly a reaction to the covert condescension and patronizing such "friendship" often masks. Their hostility also springs from the strong impression that many whites, especially the student volunteers, have used the movement chiefly as a kind of "action-therapy" for their own "hang-ups." Stokely Carmichael, who is Harlem-raised, with a degree in philosophy, and who is very much a member of this generation, speaks with intuitive insight into this phenomenon:

> Too many young, middle-class Americans, like some sort of Pepsi generation, have wanted to come alive through the black community: they've wanted to be where the action was — and the action has been in the black community.[17]

And again:

> It's important to note that those white people [who] feel alienated from white society and run into the black society ... are incapable of confronting the white society with its racism where it really does exist.[18]

The words make whites uncomfortable, but they ring true, too true to be ignored. They remind me of my chance meeting in June, 1966, at the Highlander Research and Education Center in Knoxville, Tennessee, with half a dozen white ex-SNCC staff members. They had worked in Alabama and Mississippi, and had but recently attended the conference which saw Carmichael elected SNCC Chairman. None resented the "new" policy of black organizers, and they did not feel "purged" as the press described it. But they *were* at a loss for something to do, and they had come to Highlander to think and confer with Myles Horton, the Center's veteran director.

All but one were from Northern cities, all had varying amounts of college, and all were determined to "do something" about the mess they felt their world was in. Yet, after several days of conferences, all they could think of doing was to move into Appalachia and begin organizing among the white mountain folk.

Superficially this was a plausible idea. Appalachia could certainly use some effective organizing. But the hill people of the Appalachians, especially the poorer and more rural of them, have been isolated and inbred for better than 150 years. And if the white ex-SNCCers were "outsiders" in the Black Belt, lacking ties of culture and background with Southern Negroes, they would probably be greater "outsiders" among the mountain people. If blacks were best for organizing blacks, and if white organizers in black communities perpetuated racist myths of dependence, then outsiders organizing in the tightly knit mountain communities could not but perpetuate the Appalachin varieties of the same myths. The logic of the "blacks best organize blacks, whites best organize whites" thesis seemed to lead unmistakably to the more specific conclusion that *middle-class, Northern, college-educated whites* could best organize *back home,* among middle-class, Northern, college-educated whites. I asked one of the ex-SNCCers if he did not see this implication. He nodded. "We know that's right," he said a bit ruefully, "but frankly we're just not ready to face it yet."

It is, I think, important to say here that I write of the white civil rights volunteer as an alumnus, from the inside. I left school for the South in the fall of 1964, went to jail in Selma, marched to Montgomery and taught in a Freedom School. And I know that Stokely is right about us. The "Pepsi-generation" image I find especially apt — and poignant.

This is not to imply that my — or my white co-workers' — commitment to the specific goals of the Negro struggle as we understood them was phony; on the contrary. But it *does* imply that also central to our involvement were needs and conditions which were peculiar to us and distinct from the movement's goals. Our most important need, I think, was psychological: we needed to feel as if we were doing something really significant; thus the coalitionist ideology was a necessity for us. Coalitionism was, first of all, all that most of us had ever been told about how social change comes about. It was, moreover, the only real justification for our presence in the movement: if our integrated efforts were not in fact accomplishing much, then why were we in the South? We didn't want to deal with this question, so we used the coalitionist philosophy to avoid it. The movement, after all, was the only meaningful thing we had then. And *meaning,* the experience of working in and changing *reality,* was what we wanted more than anything else.

This, I think, is what young Northern white participation in the movement was all about. Because the coalitionist idea was the only rationalization we had, we told ourselves (and others) that we were working in the South to "build the movement," in pretty much the way Bayard Rustin recommends. But because we could not seem to think of any other way to build this coalition than to go into and identify with Negro communities (some of us going to exaggerated and incongruous lengths to do so), it seems evident to me that we were indeed unable then to confront — that is, to

find meaning or to participate in changing the realities of
— our own white world back home, as the young man at Highlander admitted and Stokely Carmichael perceived. Our elders
participated pretty much on the same basis, though family
and job commitments limited the scope of their direct involvement. Both groups sought through the black struggle to
gain a conviction that they were contributing substantially to
real social change.

Can this be the reason for the liberal rejection and dis-
tortion of Black Power? We liberals cling to the movement; we
cannot *let* it say to us, as these new voices are saying, "You are
irrelevant to our struggle, and you even are beginning to get
in our way." If necessary, it seems, whites preserve their
illusion of importance by exaggerating the peripheral outbursts of hostility into Rustin's "no-win" "strategy of shock,"
where the white liberal is the "main enemy," whose hypocrisy "above all" must be exposed.[19] But such an understanding
of Black Power is a gross misunderstanding, one that suggests
the condition of the whites at Highlander, inability to face
Black Power's *real* implications.

But now it seems we must give up our old illusions and
face these implications. We cannot find the meaning we seek
for our lives in our previous participation in the Negro
movement, because the meaning *is not there.* We are indeed
irrelevant to any strategy for real social change, because
*liberals today do not in fact have signficant power in our
society* — power in Carmichael's sense of being able to
move institutions so that people's needs are "spoken
to." We have examined the institutional elements of the
grand coalition — labor, corporate-academic liberalism, and
churches — finding them seriously and basically compromised
with the status quo against real solutions to the problems of
America's oppressed black minority, and finding that liberals
within them generally do not have significant control of the
institutions anyway. We have looked at the coalition's performance — and we have seen that so far it has not been able
to "deliver the goods" of change except for a small minority
of Negroes, and it has won *them* only crumbs. The coalition's

prospects are not heartening either: such events as the failure of organized labor to win repeal of section 14B of the Taft-Hartley Act — a struggle which determines whether or not the South will be organized — during the 89th Congress, supposedly the most liberal since 1933, suggests to me that labor (the coalition's wealthiest and weightiest segment), can't even deliver on its *own* program when the chips are down.

We went South, then, because we could see no way of making our own lives meaningful by working for change in our white world. Many of us still can't. This feeling of powerlessness, strongest among the young New Left radicals, has an objective basis in the patterns of life in the middle-class white world. The basic pattern is as follows. Each June a college generation graduates, and immediately most of it moves into the "junior executive" or technical departments of major institutions, the jobs for which they have been trained in college. These jobs become the effective centers around which all major aspects of their lives are organized — more important than politics, more important than religion, in many cases more important than families. In thirty to forty years most of these people will retire from these institutions, after having risen several appropriate rungs on the various hierarchical ladders and perhaps having assumed a certain quantitative amount of responsibility. But only a tiny handful of them will have gained any *real power* in determining the overall direction and objectives of the institution to which they have dedicated all their years, nor will most of them even have had a *voice* in selecting those who did wield such power. The majority of them, during their whole careers, will have carried out or made possible the policies that were determined by those who did have institutional power. This pattern is very much the same whether the institution involved is a business corporation, church, or labor union bureauracy, university, military or government agency. Most liberals today, as I mentioned earlier, are working for, and thus are limited by, such organizations and their powerlessness.

Much of the young radical and New Left phenomena

among white students is a reaction against just such a type of career, to which they have been oriented all their lives. Most students, it is true, are still content to seek only the most comfortable niche available within the system; but the young radicals reject the system as being dehumanizing to those within it (no matter how well paid they may be) and exploitative of those subject to it, Negroes at home and non-white masses abroad in places like Africa, Latin America, and Southeast Asia.

This view has much in common with Black Power. Both postulate powerlessness, inability to move institutions, or to "speak to needs" as a basic characteristic of their constituencies. They differ in the point of view from which they see the situation: for blacks, powerlessness is accompanied by overt oppression, exploitation, discrimination and brutality; for whites, powerlessness can be comfortable, well paid and tempting. White radicals who "cop out" and join the system usually can find a well-upholstered place waiting for them, complete with the coalitionist's illusion of importance; few blacks can join the system even if they want to. But to repeat, the central fact about each community is that *it does not control the institutions around and through which its life is organized and controlled.* Organized labor comes closest to having such a base, but its own internal problems, as we have seen, keep it from using this potential for something other than a narrow version of its own self-interest.

Until the liberal community now in the employ of corporations, unions, universities, and churches develops — as Black Power insists that Negroes must develop — an economic base which it can control, which can support the community substantially, and which can confront other power groups as equals, its power will remain illusory. It will remain the kind that can bring Senators and Presidents to speak at graduations and conventions, but which cannot move institutions and pass and enforce legislation meaningful to its interests. Such a community's cries to the blacks for support of its "grand coalition" will continue to lack credibility.

The anger and self-castigation that Black Power spokesmen have directed at Negroes for their cultural self-denial and especially the dissipation of their resources in white-owned exploitative businesses could, it seems to me, be usefully imitated by liberals. We smoke, and our dollars support that pillar of Southern racism, the tobacco industry; without thinking about it, we buy Shick razor blades, our wives pick up Hunt's tomato products (not to mention Welch candies), thus adding to the coffers that help shore up the right-wing; we buy bananas harvested by a United Fruit Company that for decades has contributed to the maintenance of neo-feudalism in Central America; we buy other fruit picked by the serfs in our own migrant labor camps; our comfortable middle-class salaries are deposited in the banks whose loans can bolster the economy of racist South Africa but can't help rebuild our own slums.

The list could be multiplied at length. The point is that in their economic existence as consumers, savers, and investors, liberals pass most of their wealth back into the hands of businesses that are solidly embedded in the status quo; many of them are architects and direct beneficiaries of the racism and reaction we then verbally and in our journals so deplore. This dissipation of resources not only profits these institutions; it also keeps us powerless by keeping us from controlling the uses of our resources, which in turn prevents us from developing a political force that is really responsibile to us.

The encounter between the Lowndes County sharecropper and the SNCC worker, illustrates the power situation faced by liberals today. Until we can offer politicians "a place to live and some land to work," we cannot expect to tell them how to vote. And since I have drawn the comparison between the liberal community and the Lowndes County Freedom Party, it is logical that I also see the Party's present course — the development of an economic base independent of its opponents — as the foundation and prerequisite for an effective politics of liberal change in race or any other matter of liberal concern. Only such a base can be potentially "relevant" (as either friend or foe) to Black Power's organized Negro communities. In addition, I find the cooperative enterprise fully as appropriate to the development of such a liberal base as it is to the development of power in Negro communities. Cooperatives in urban areas have in fact flourished best in middle-class, highly educated areas, such as the university city of Berkeley, California.

The development of such a base seems to me to be the first priority for a serious liberal strategy. For though I have differed with Bayard Rustin profoundly, I think he was right when he said that even an organized Negro (or in this case, liberal) community alone could not muster the force necessary for all the change it desired. An independent liberal power base would, however, make feasible Carmichael's "meaningful political alliances on specific issues," and would have much more power for both sides than what now passes as a grand liberal coalition.

Chapter Four
THE LIBERAL TASKS

The development of a liberal-radical power base could do
more than vitalize the Negro-white coalition that white liberals seem to need so badly; it could also begin to speak to the
condition of powerlessness that underlies the coalitionist's insecurity and forms the driving impulse of the New Left revolt.
It could, that is, begin to give us something *meaningful* to do
in our white world. By creating a credible alternative within
the white world to the middle-class organizational treadmill,
it would become possible for whites to "come alive" without
fleeing into a futile identification with the Negro community.
They could then work with blacks, where appropriate, on a
more truly equal basis. This is, after all, the only way cultural
barriers between the two groups can begin to fall while each
preserves its integrity.

Self-Examination
But this strategy also poses challenges to white liberals,
especially younger New Left radicals. It challenges them first
to abandon their illusions about themselves. This means that
older liberals must give up the idea that, because they have
degrees, hold "responsible" positions, make good salaries, and
get courteous replies when they write their congressmen, they
therefore have "power." Younger radicals must get over the
impression that because they are angry, alienated, scornful
of "the establishment," presumably immune from its blandish-
ments, and committed to "radical" action, they therefore are

on the front lines of social change. Adult liberalism and youthful activism today are both, as we have seen, mostly a lot of sound and fury, signifying little that is substantial. Their present powerless state is, I am convinced, the most *important* and most *difficult* fact about their lives for liberals — old and young — to grasp and maintain. The fact is important because it is *basic* to strategy for real change; it is difficult to keep before us because the whole opinion-making apparatus of the status quo has been mobilized to convince us otherwise. Many big corporations, sensing a trend among college students away from the cogwheel careers they offer, have mounted a vigorous public relations counterattack in their recruiting pitches to college seniors. One such pitch runs as follows:

> Want to change the world? Join the Peace Corps... or join General Electric.
> ... all it takes is brains, imagination, drive and a fairly rugged constitution. These qualities can get you a job with General Electric — or with the Peace Corps.
> If you choose the Peace Corps, we'll understand. But when the day comes that you leave the Corps, remember us. You'll still be young, and at General Electric, the young men are important men.[1]

Another G.E. ad asks: "Are you discontented enough to work for G.E.?"[2] Western Electric recently enticed the class of '67 with an ad under the headline, "It's trade-in time for tired old myths," which read in part:

> Like the one about business. Especially big business. That it is beyond the rugged individualist's wildest daydreams to enter this holy of holies because he'll lose something that's very sacred — like his independence.
> Sure, it can happen. If a guy or gal *wants* to hide, or just get by, or not accept responsibilities, or challenges.
> We're not omniscient enough or stupid enough to speak for all business, but at a company like Western Electric, bright ideas are not only welcome, they are encouraged. And no door is shut. Create a little stir, go ahead, upset an old applecart (we replace shibboleths at a terrific pace — we have to as manufacturing and supply unit of the Bell System)....

...if you consider yourself an individual *now*, odds are ten to one that you'll keep your individuality. And cherish it. And watch it grow. Even at big, big Western Electric.

You know, that's the only way we'd want you to feel. If you feel like coming in with us.[3]

I expect this kind of campaigning will win back many who are skeptical but lack the wherewithal to seek alternatives; but the converts will learn soon enough that this "new look" in recruiting has not altered the reality of corporate operations. And any sincere young activist would have to be extremely gullible to fall for such sophistries.

MEANINGFUL ACTION

The second challenge to liberals is to stop talking and begin to take meaningful action toward developing such a power base for their community. Older liberals, who tend to be "tied down" somewhat by family and other obligations, must figure out how to withdraw their money and abilities as much as possible from status quo institutions and rechannel the *bulk* of them into the development and support of independent-base institutions. The New Left, to make much of this strategy, must (horror of horrors!) go back to school. Such a proposal will no doubt stamp me in some "radical" minds as a hypocritical sellout, trying to put them in some kind of trick. But it seems obvious to me that to build a real base, liberals *must* develop a large pool of people with a variety of skills. A national cooperative organization, for example, owns an oil refinery in Kansas, and the refinery is *not* run by alienation, or even commitment and participatory democracy, but by *skills,* highly technical skills that people do not learn by dropping out to organize in the Black Belt. This is not meant to imply that it is not worthwhile either to drop out of school or to organize in the Black Belt; I have done both, and it is only because I have that I feel qualified to suggest that they are a *stage* in radical development, not the end of an honest man's search for meaning. We must go back to school because our liberal-radical job is not to *escape* "the system," but to humanize it. And to humanize it we must learn where it is going and how to run it. It is clear, for example, that computers, teaching machines and TV could, instead of turning universities into factories, possibly remake them into places where a real community of scholars is possible even for great numbers; but it will take men with radical vision *and* know-how to harness these devices and make such communities a reality. If the New Left took over the universities tomorrow, would there be enough such men to do the job?

This is not a pseudo-liberal plea for "working within the system for change," in the manner of a student I met at Yale who planned to become the head of General Motors and *then* do "liberal things." By the time he gets to the top of G.M., I am quite sure he will be no more liberal than the Company's other presidents. Yet those who at the opposite extreme can see no way whatever to preserve their integrity while having anything at all to do with "the system" and its instruments, have in effect admitted "the system's" omnipotence; for if they even touch it, they say, it will absorb them. They are actually at "the system's" mercy, because their whole stance is dictated by it. They have also missed the point, because "the system's" evil is in its use of technology, and not the technology itself.

THE RELEVANCE OF SYSTEM AND HISTORY

Another challenge the liberal-radical strategy throws down, again especially to the New Left, is that of trying to see our society and our own world *whole,* which implies coming to terms with ideology. Edward M. Keating, former publisher of *Ramparts* magazine and New Left candidate for Congress in 1966, made a statement in the *Saturday Review* which is revealing in this connection:

> The end sought [by the New Left] is not a new system, since systems — whether the current one in this country, those in communist countries, or for that matter, any system of the past — are irrelevant. What *is* relevant is justice. Whereas the "Old Left" sought economic justice, the "New Left" has a far broader concern that encompasses social, economic, and

political justice. Its ultimate goal is peace — domestic and international — and peace is impossible without justice.[4]

Certainly Mr. Keating has captured the mood of the New Left, with its healthy disrespect for obsolete dogmas of another day, its scorn for the substitution of interminable and pointless "academic research" for real action, and its assertion that values are not so very difficult to understand. All this is agreeable, but too abstract. Real societies cannot operate on mere abstractions any more than a cooperative refinery can be operated by committed radicals who know nothing of chemistry. And in real societies, the question of how to make an economic system, or an educational system, or a political system *just* is not a simple matter, and those who undertake such tasks must often make important, difficult, technical choices, choices that have to be organized in some pattern, some *system*.

The fact is that systems *are* relevant, because it is through systems that men — honest, radical men — have tried to see societies whole so as to bring justice into men's dealings with each other. That's what Plato's *Republic* is about, and Adam Smith and the Federalist Papers, and Marx; and it is ultimately what we are about as well. Moreover, liberalism and radicalism have histories, just as do the problems they wish to tackle and the systems they consider irrelevant; and we are simply crippling ourselves if we do not try to understand these histories and their meaning — if only, as someone has said, *to rid ourselves of them.* The ideology of liberal coalition rationalizes itself with a view of how the system works and changes; my critique of this ideology is based on another view of how the system works and changes; *any* strategy presumes a view of how a society works and changes, and that is a system.

Something of what recent liberal-radical history might teach us is evoked in a recent article by John Fischer, an executive of *Harper's* magazine, entitled "Letter to a New Leftist, From a Tired Liberal." It is excerpted at some length below because I found it very sobering and provocative:

> There are ... explanations for the older liberals' hesitancy — which seems to you so unpardonable — about your

[The New Left's] causes. The radicals of the thirties (when nearly all of us were radicals of some kind) invested a lot of emotion and sweat in such causes. Some of them succeeded beyond our wildest hopes; but others, even when successful, did not produce quite the results we had expected.

Consider the labor unions, for instance. To us it seemed self-evident that the quickest route to universal reform was to muster all the unorganized workers into strong unions. They would then form the backbone of a liberal political movement, something like the Labor Party in England (which then looked a lot more revolutionary than it does today). The unions would pressure Congress into a radical restructuring of the economy, so that unemployment would become impossible. They would abolish racial discrimination in jobs and schools and housing. They would see to it that we kept out of all wars. Under the leadership of the intellectuals, organized labor — with its newfound freedom, leisure, and money — would rejuvenate the arts and theater, toning up the soul and muscle of the whole American society.

With that vision beckoning us, a good many young people worked hard (and at some economic risk) to build the new unions. . . . We helped pass the Wagner Act, minimum-wage laws, and a long list of other legislation to help the working man. We won nearly all the battles — but the victory didn't turn out to be quite as glorious as advertised.

Instead of becoming the shock troops of liberalism, the unions (with very few exceptions) quickly petrified into lumps of reaction and special privilege. I don't need to tell you that some of them — notably in the construction trades — are the stubbornest opponents of integration; that they have no use for intellectuals, no interest in the arts, no cultural aspirations higher than the bowling alley; that none of their aged leaders, except Walter Reuther, has entertained a fresh political idea in twenty years. . . .

This is the main reason, I think, why the middle-aged no longer plunge into radical movements with a zeal equal to yours. They are not indifferent and they haven't sold out. They have just gone astray so often on the road to the New Jerusalem that they want to make very sure of the road map before embarking on another march. . . .

What I am describing, of course, is that prime target of your derision, the Tired Liberal; remember that he earned his weariness by years of aching labor, and many a disappointment — and that you may not always be immune to such weariness yourself. . . .

If you seriously hope to overcome organized power, you can do it only by organizing a power base of your own. You will also find — alas — that it has to have some kind of hierarchy, some degree of discipline, a considerable amount of continuity and finance. "Participatory democracy" is a splendid ideal, but I think you already are discovering that it isn't very effective unless somebody takes the responsibility for drafting a program, seeing to it that decisions get made, and then making sure that they are carried out. . . .

What this country needs is radicals who will stay that way — regardless of the creeping years, the inevitable blunders, defeats and combat fatigue. For the rate of change in the world today is unimaginably faster than ever before and we can hope to survive in reasonably good shape only if we change our human institutions fast enough to keep up. This means constant radical reexamination of everything in sight, from political system to sex habits — radical in the old sense of going to the roots. . . .

You and your comrades-in-arms will keep trying, I hope, even when you are long past thirty and a younger generation of radicals is watching you with impatience and pity. For the only corruption you really need to fear is the corruption of despair.[5]

One of the most important insights we can gain from Mr. Fischer, it seems to me, is a sense of the passage of time, the consciousness that, whether we like to admit it or not, even Lyndon Johnson was once a brash and enthusiastic New Dealer Congressman and men like Hubert Humphrey, as we suggested earlier, once spent many years fighting doggedly for causes that in days gone by were as "radical" as they were hopeless. Even more important than this perspective on our elders, however, is the perspective older liberals like Fischer can give us on *ourselves*. He remarks in connection with the Berkeley-born New Left slogan "Never trust anybody over 30," that while he does not disagree with the slogan, "if you will forgive me for mentioning such a grisly fact, you will soon — ah, how soon — be over thirty yourself."[6] It seems fair to observe that few young radicals really believe yet that they will ever get much older than they are, or that time could change the way they see things. This is a common youthful delusion, I suspect; but when we get over it, we will need to learn, among other things, to think and act in terms of change that may take years and decades to accomplish, years and decades that are likely to change us as much as we can change them.

Along with the realization that we, like every other generation, can expect to get old, comes the equally disheartening discovery that, if our radical forebears, even in victory, were still unable to avoid making mistakes, it is quite possible that we will leave posterity a new set of problems, some the result of our mistakes and others just the needs of a new set of conditions. A far-sighted observer, for example, could probably have foreseen what would come of the organizing successes of the 30's; but even seeing this future, he would probably have had to go out and organize *anyway*, because there was simply no real alternative *for his generation*.

Similarly, while there does not seem to be any alternative to the development of a liberal power base such as we discussed earlier and to which Fischer referred, there is no guarantee that such a base, once developed, could avoid becoming just another vested interest. But if this did happen, it would then be the task of the new generation to supplant it. How many of us, carrying our antiwar placards, recall that in the late eighteenth and early nineteenth centuries our own new United States was feared and abhorred all over royal and imperial Europe as the center of subversion and the prime exporter of dangerous and revolutionary notions about democracy and human rights? All our white immigrant forebears didn't come here for nothing.

The prospect that today's radicalism may be inadequate to tomorrow's needs does not seem at all depressing to me: rather, I suppose it is what we must expect from life as long as man's nature is imperfect and change is a basic characteristic of the world he lives in. We have our job to do; the next generation will rightly have its own tasks. Our job is described by Kenneth Clark:

> The problem posed for Negroes and those whites who are committed to actual social change as a reality and not

a mere social posture is that of identifying, mobilizing, and using that power necessary to translate laws into meaningful changes in the day-to-day lives of those whom the laws are intended to protect.[7]

Dr. Clark's remarks apply equally well to efforts for the benefit of blacks or whites. He also alludes to the pitfall that white middle-class liberals and radicals must avoid above all: that of accepting a *posture* of social change instead of its reality. The organized status quo today is peddling many such illusory postures, in the hope of diluting, "co-opting" and buying off the liberal and radical elements of our generation. The test of our radicalism will be in whether we can effectively resist and offer viable alternatives to these efforts. It is a job that requires all the maturity, courage, and skill we have or can hope to get.

CONCLUSION

Throughout these meditations, the most evocative image of Black Power for me has been that of the emerging *manhood* of a race. Several observers besides those we have already heard from have alluded to such an image. Richard Bone, reviewing *The Autobiography of Malcolm X* for *The New York Times* had this to say:

> "Freedom Now!" is addressed to whites; it is a shorthand version of "Give us our freedom now!" But "Black Power!" is addressed to Negroes; it is a call to mobilize their full social weight for the achievement of certain goals. The essence of the shift is psychological. It has nothing to do with black supremacy, but much to do with manhood and self-reliance.[1]

The Rev. George Kalbfleisch, in a letter to the *Times,* drew a somewhat similar comparison:

> It was a personally humanizing act for the Jew under the Nazis actually to lay claim to his being a Jew. It is a personally humanizing act for the Black Man under the whites actually to lay claim to his being black.[2]

C. E. Vanderwarker, Jr., also wrote the *Times* about the meaning of the emerging concept:

> The Negro has surfaced from under the confining and directing hand of a white society and will now conduct his struggle as he sees fit. This is not separatism, nor a prelude to widespread violence, nor a "taking of the law into their own hands"; this is simply a "taking of themselves into their own hands" — an assertion that the Negro is finally able

106

to act as a man, not as the mythical creation bordering on invisibility which he was previously.[3]

It is this feeling of "taking one's life in one's own hands" that communicates best the meaning I have sensed in Black Power. Such a taking over is the core definition of manhood for most of us, I think. Certainly it was this vision on the part of oppressed Negroes, who without weapons or resources acted to remove barriers to this self-direction, which first caught the attention of young, discontented whites. And it was the development of the blacks' consciousness both of the magnitude of these barriers and the radical nature of the action needed to meet them which made it necessary for Negroes to redefine the role of white "friends."

I am convinced that on the other side of the white liberal coin of social-institutional powerlessness lies an existential situation identical to that which produced Black Power: that of a search for a way or ways to take oneself and one's life "in our own hands," and to do so against large, even overwhelming obstacles. The two situations also seem to me similar in another respect, one which few of us have yet to confront in the manner that Negroes have had to confront it. Mr. Walter Palmer, a Philadelphia (Pa.) Negro, put his finger on this when he told a white audience:

> It is fear, fear for their lives which keeps white people from going back and dealing with racism in the white community, because they *know* what power this structure has, and how they're a minority in it, and that the structure could do away with them just as it has done away with anybody else who threatens it.[4]

Few whites among this generation really know just how dangerous it can be for a person seriously to try to discover all the bitter truth about his world and himself, and to try to take his life "in his own hands" on the basis of this truth and not on the comfortable lies we normally exist by. We have not yet experienced this fear; but I doubt if we can avoid it much longer, because some members of our generation (Malcolm X was one, even though he was older) have come close to discovering some of this truth and have been trying to act on it. It will probably take all our courage just to assimilate some of the things we may learn. We will need a secular form of "grace" to act on them. Suppose, for example, that it is true, as Carmichael has asserted, that for "racism to die, a totally new America must be born."[5] How many of us white radicals, raised in comfort on the fruits of this racism, can really believe that the death of racism requires a new America? And how many of us who believe it can actually forsake our color-guaranteed access to these fruits and begin to act meaningfully on such a belief? Or in our own context: How many of us are prepared to pursue our analysis of the system we have criticized *wherever* it may lead? And to *act* on what we find? And how many of us are prepared to confront the reactions of people and institutions whose very reasons for existence we may be led to challenge?

I consider it nonsense to expect that such a redistribution of power as is implicitly the objective of the New Left will be accomplished without major upheavals and long, bitter struggles — struggles that have yet to begin. But only as we seriously lay claim to our right to take "in our own hands" our lives both individual and social, can we find *our* manhood, our own "personally humanizing act" that can give meaning both to us and to our struggle.

NOTES

CHAPTER ONE: THE ELEMENTS OF BLACK POWER

[1]Bayard Rustin, "Black Power and Coalition Politics," *Commentary*, Vol. 41, No. 9 (Sept. 1966), p. 35.

[2]Lerone Bennett, Jr., *Before the Mayflower*, rev. ed. (Chicago, 1964), p. 93.

[3]Charles Silberman, *Crisis in Black and White* (New York, 1964), p. 89.

[4]R. A. Cloward and F. F. Piven, "Desegregated Housing," *The New Republic*, Dec. 17, 1966, p. 19.

[5]"The Lost Agency," *The Nation*, Dec. 19, 1966, pp. 660-1.

[6]Kenneth Clark, *Dark Ghetto* (New York, 1965), p. 35.

[7]*Ibid.*, p. 13.

[8]John Benson, "Interview with Stokely Carmichael," *The Militant*, May 23, 1966.

[9]Rustin, *op. cit.*, p. 37.

[10]James Farmer, *Freedom — When?* (New York, 1965), p. 85.

[11]Whitney Young, *To Be Equal* (New York, 1964), pp. 252, 18-19, 250.

[12]Elsie Archer, *Let's Face It* (Philadelphia, 1959), p. 12.

[13]Archer, *op. cit.*, pp. 54-6.

[14]*Ibid.*, p. 56.

[15]Carmichael, speech at Mt. Holyoke College, Nov. 17, 1966.

[16]Farmer, *op. cit.*, p. 87 (emphasis in original).

[17]Silberman, *op. cit.*, pp. 165-6.

[18]*Ibid.*, p. 166.

[19]Carmichael, *op. cit.*

[20]Malcolm X, *Autobiography* (New York, 1964), p. 41.

[21]*Ibid.*, p. 53.

[22]*Ibid.*, p. 54.

[23]Clark, *op. cit.*, pp. 64-5.

[24]"If You're Black, Stay Back," *Trans-ACTION*, Vol. 4, No. 1 (Nov., 1966), p. 2.

[25]Benson, *op. cit.*

[26]Carmichael, *op. cit.* (emphasis in original).

[27]Kenneth Stampp, *The Peculiar Institution* (New York, 1956), p. 145.

[28]Clark, *op. cit.*

29Carmichael, *op. cit.*

30Carmichael, in *The Amsterdam News,* July 16, 1966.

31Carmichael, "What We Want," *The New York Review of Books,* Sept. 22, 1966, p. 6.

32See "Dr. King Clarifies His Racial Stand," *The New York Times,* Oct. 17, 1966, p. 42, and King, "Black Power," *The Progressive,* Nov. 1966, p. 15; cf. also a fund-raising letter sent from the Southern Christian Leadership Conference under Dr. King's signature, Nov. 1966.

33John F. Phillips, "Black Power," *The Scarlet and Black,* Grinnell College, Sept. 9, 1966, p. 8.

34Carmichael, "What We Want," p. 6.

35*Ibid.,* p. 5.

36Benson, *op. cit.*

37See our discussion of the Child Development Group of Mississippi, pp. 69ff.

38See "Douglas Runs on 18-year Record of Fighting for Civil Rights," *Jet,* Nov. 10, 1966, p. 8.

39Carmichael, speech at Mt. Holyoke.

40Clark, *op. cit.,* p. 34.

41Farmer, *op. cit.,* p. 100.

42Robert Parris (nee Moses), "Nonviolence in the Ghetto," *The New Radicals,* ed. Paul Jacobs and Saul Landau (New York, 1966), p. 124.

43Palmer, speech to Workshop on Black Power of Metropolitan Associates of Philadelphia, Valley Forge, Pa., Oct. 14, 1966.

44Baldwin, in Silberman, *op. cit.,* p. 153.

45*Meet the Press,* Aug. 21, 1966. Text printed by Merkle Press, Washington, D.C., p. 22.

46*Ibid.,* p. 26.

47*Ibid.,* p. 23.

48Clark, *op. cit.,* p. 16.

49Jackson, quoted in *The Amsterdam News,* Aug. 27, 1966.

50Carmichael, interview with K. Nordin, *Christian Science Monitor,* July 23, 1966, p. 10.

51Carmichael, speech at Mt. Holyoke.

52Benson, *op. cit.*

53See Robert Analavage, "Lowndes Party Girds for Future," *The Southern Patriot,* Dec. 1966, p. 1.

54Lerone Bennett, "Stokely Carmichael: Architect of Black Power," *Ebony,* Sept. 1966, p. 26.

55Barry Sheppard, "Interview With CORE Leader," *The Militant,* Aug. 8, 1966, p. 5.

56Carmichael, "What We Want," p. 6.

57"A 'Freedom Budget' for all Americans," A. Philip Randolph Institute (New York, 1966).

58During a debate with Bayard Rustin on "The Future of the Negro Movement," at Hunter College, New York City, Dec. 14, 1966, Carmichael made remarks to this effect in response to a question concerning why SNCC had endorsed, then withdrawn its name from the Freedom Budget.

[59]Carmichael, "What We Want," p. 6.

[60]Rustin made this remark at the debate referred to in note 58.

[61]Dr. Breeden made this statement in a speech to the Workshop on Black Power referred to in note 43.

[62]James Baldwin and Budd Schulberg, "Dialog in Black and White," *Playboy*, Dec. 1966, p. 282.

[63]Rustin, "Black Power and Coalition Politics," in *Commentary*, Vol. 41, No. 9 (Sept. 1966).

[64]Cook, in *New South*, Vol. 21, No. 3 (Summer 1966).

[65]Wilkins, in *The Crisis*, Vol. 73, No. 7 (Aug.-Sept. 1966), p. 354.

[66]Quoted in Rowan, *Ebony*, Vol. 22, No. 1 (Nov. 1966).

[67]Rowan, *op. cit.*, p. 34.

[68]*Ibid.*, p. 28.

[69]Cook, *op. cit.*, p. 59.

[70]Wilkins, *op. cit.*, p. 354.

[71]Editorial, "The Politics of Frustration," *The New York Times*, Aug. 7, 1966.

[72]Wechsler, " 'Killers of the Dream,' " *The Progressive*, Vol. 30, No. 12 (Dec. 1966), pp. 12-13.

[73]Cook, *op. cit.*, p. 60.

[74]Quoted in Rowan, *op. cit*, p. 28.

[75]Carmichael, speech at Mt. Holyoke.

[76]Carmichael, "What We Want," p. 7.

[77]Quoted in Paul Good, "A White Look at Black Power," *The Nation*, Aug. 18, 1966, p. 114.

[78]Bennett, *op. cit.*, p. 28.

[79]See Bernard Weinraub, "The Brilliancy of Black," *Esquire*, Jan. 1967, p. 132, for Harlem and Newark; Gordon Bailey, "Big Rally in Watts Hears Carmichael," *The Militant*, Dec. 5, 1966, p. 1, for Los Angeles; and John Sinclair, "Stokely in Detroit: Who's Afraid of Black Power?" *The Fifth Estate*, Oct. 16-31, p. 1, for Detroit.

[80]Rowan, *op. cit.*, p. 32.

[81]Carmichael, speech at Mt. Holyoke.

[82]*Ibid.*

[83]Malcolm X, *op. cit.*, p. 313.

[84]"Excerpts From Paper on Which the 'Black Power' Philosophy Is Based," *The New York Times*, Aug. 5, 1966, p. 10.

[85]C. Eric Lincoln, *The Black Muslims in America* (Boston, 1961), p. 228.

[86]See my examples of pejorative associations with blackness in common slang, above, p. 29.

[87]Silberman, *op. cit.*, p. 49.

[88]"Excerpts," *Times*, Aug. 5, 1966.

[89]Carmichael, in his Mt. Holyoke speech, specifically rejected a conspiracy theory, and suggested that the basis of this racism was rather pervasive within the life-patterns of virtually (if not all) whites in this country.

[90]See above, the section "Despair: A Constant Shadow," pp. 33ff.

CHAPTER TWO: THE IDEOLOGY OF THE LIBERAL COALITION

[1]"Excerpts From the Vice-President's Speech to NAACP Convention," *The New York Times*, July 7, 1966.

2 *Ibid.*

3Quoted in *The Crisis,* Aug.-Sept. 1966, p. 362 (emphasis added).

4Quoted in *The Amsterdam News,* Oct. 29, 1966.

5Column in *The Amsterdam News,* Sept. 10, 1966.

6Column in *The Amsterdam News,* Oct. 15, 1966.

7"Keynote Address to Policy Conference, March on Washington Movement, 1962," in August Meier and Francis Broderick, *Negro Protest Thought in The Twentieth Century* (Indianapolis, 1965), pp. 203-4.

8In *Commentary,* Feb. 1965. Reprinted in Jacobs and Landau, *The New Radicals* (New York, 1966), pp. 295-310.

9In *Commentary,* Vol. 41, No. 9 (Sept. 1966), pp. 35-40.

10Jacobs and Landau, *Radicals,* p. 296.

11*Ibid.,* p. 298.

12*Ibid.,* pp. 305-6.

13*Ibid.,* p. 306.

14*Ibid.,* p. 301.

15*Ibid.,* p. 303.

16*Ibid.*

17*Ibid.*

18*Ibid.,* p. 307.

19*Ibid.,* p. 306.

20Rustin, "Black Power and Coalition Politics," *Commentary,* Vol. 41, No. 9 (Sept. 1966), p. 39.

21*Ibid.,* p. 35.

22*Ibid.,* p. 38.

23*Ibid.*

24*Ibid.,* p. 36.

25*Ibid.*

26*Ibid.,* p. 38.

27*Ibid.*

28*Ibid.,* p. 39.

29*Ibid.*

30*Ibid.*

31*Ibid.,* p. 36.

32*Ibid.,* p. 40.

33*Ibid.,* p. 37 (emphasis in original).

34*Ibid.*

35PL 88-352, 88th Congress, H.R. 7152, July 2, 1964.

36See the statement of Leon Keyserling before the Subcommittee on the War on Poverty Program of the House Committee on Education and Labor; 89th Congress, April 30, 1965, pp. 735ff.

37Rustin, "Black Power and Coalition Politics," in *Commentary,* Vol. 41, No. 9 (Sept. 1966), p. 40.

38This information is taken from the story "HEW Learns a Lesson," in *Newsweek,* Oct. 18, 1966, p. 98.

39A good summary of the battle is in "Shriver Comes Across," *The New Republic,* Vol. 156, No. 1 (Jan. 7, 1967), p. 10.

40Cf. Gene Roberts, "Shriver Refuses Dr. King's Appeal," *The New York Times,* Oct. 25, 1966, p. 32.

41*New York Times,* Oct. 19, 1966, p. 35.

42James A. Wechsler, "Labor In Retreat: The AFL-CIO Tragedy," *The Progressive*, Vol. 31, No. 1 (Jan. 1966), p. 14.

43David Danzig, "The Meaning of Negro Strategy," *Commentary* (Feb. 1964), p. 46.

44Clark, *Dark Ghetto*, pp. 41-2.

45Gene Marine, "I've Got Nothing Against the Colored, Understand," *Ramparts*, Vol. 5, No. 5 (Nov. 1966), p. 15.

46*Ibid.*, p. 17

47Clark, *op cit.*, pp. 42-3.

48*Ibid.*, pp. 43-5.

49Young, *To Be Equal*, p. 71.

50"The Lost Agency," *The Nation*, Vol. 203, No. 21 (Dec. 19, 1966), pp. 660-1.

51Silberman, *Crisis in Black and White*, p. 216.

52Jacobs and Landau, *Radicals*, p. 307.

53Wechsler, *op. cit.*, p. 15.

54C. W. Mills, *The Power Elite* (New York, 1959), p. 149.

55Hans Morgenthau, "Truth and Power," *The New Republic*, Vol. 155, No. 22 (Nov. 26, 1966), pp. 10, 12-13.

56See Frederic Heimberger, *Daedalus*, Fall, 1964, pp. 1093ff.

57Jacobs and Landau, *Radicals*, pp. 306-7.

58Jeffrey Hadden and Raymond Rymph, "The Marching Ministers," *Trans-ACTION*, Vol. 3, No. 5 (Sept.-Oct. 1966), pp. 38-41.

59*Ibid.*, pp. 38-9.

60*Ibid.*, p. 41.

61*The Christian Century*, May 13, 1964 (emphasis mine).

62Rustin, "Black Power and Coalition Politics," *Commentary*, Vol. 41, No. 9 (Sept. 1966), p. 35.

64Humphrey, speech to Workshop on Black Power, Valley Forge, Pa. Oct. 14, 1966; See notes 43 and 61 to Chapter 1.

65Carmichael, speech at Mt. Holyoke.

66Rustin, "Black Power and Coalition Politics," *Commentary*, Vol. 41, No. 9 (Sept. 1966), p. 40.

CHAPTER THREE: LIBERALS AND BLACK POWER

1Barry Sheppard, "Interview With CORE Leader," *The Militant*, Aug. 8, 1966, p. 5.

2Carmichael, speech at Mt. Holyoke.

3Carmichael, *Jet*, June 2, 1966, p. 9.

4"Interview With Stokely Carmichael," *The Movement*, March, 1966, p. 1.

5"Coming: Wide-Open Split Among Negro Leaders," *The National Observer*, Oct. 10, 1966, p. 1.

6*Ibid.*, p. 10 .

6aCf. *Newsday*, Vol. 27, No. 101 (Jan. 3, 1967), p. 61, and *The New York Times*, Jan. 8, 1967 p. 54.

7Rowan, "Crisis in Civil Rights Leadership," *Ebony*, Vol. XXII, No. 1 (Nov. 1966), p. 28.

8*The Amsterdam News*, Nov. 5, 1966.

9C. Eric Lincoln, *The Black Muslims in America*, p. 64.

10*Newsweek*, Nov. 7, 1966, p. 37.

[11]Robert Analavage, "Lowndes Party Girds for Future," *The Southern Patriot*, Vol. 24, No. 11 (Dec. 1966), p. 8.

[12]*Ibid.*

[13]Clark, *Dark Ghetto*, p. 28.

[14]"Growl of the Panther," *Newsweek*, May 30, 1966, p. 33.

[15]See Jerry Voorhis, *American Cooperatives* (New York, 1961).

[16]See *They All Endorse Cooperatives* (Chicago, The Cooperative League of the U.S.A.).

[17]Carmichael, "What We Want," *The New York Review of Books*, Sept. 22, 1966, p. 7.

[18]Carmichael, speech at Mt. Holyoke.

[19]Jacobs and Landau, *Radicals*, p. 303.

CHAPTER FOUR: THE LIBERAL TASKS

[1]Quoted from an ad in *The Colorado State University Collegian*, Nov. 3, 1966.

[2]*The Collegian*, Nov. 18, 1966.

[3]*The Collegian*, Nov. 7, 1966.

[4]Keating, *Saturday Review*, Sept. 24, 1966, pp. 25-26.

[5]*Harper's*, Vol. 232, No. 1390 (March, 1966), pp. 16-28.

[6]*Ibid.*, p. 16.

[7]Clark, *Dark Ghetto*, p. 203.

CONCLUSION

[1]Bone, "A Black Man's Quarrel With the Christian God," *The New York Times Book Review*, Sept. 11, 1966, p. 14.

[2]Letter to the Editor, *The New York Times*, Aug. 19, 1966.

[3]Letter to the Editor, *The New York Times*, July 23, 1966.

[4]Workshop on Black Power, Oct. 14, 1966, Valley Forge, Pa.

[5]Carmichael, "What We Want," *The New York Review of Books*, Sept. 22, 1966, p. 6.

Bibliography

Part I of this bibliography lists materials that are directly concerned with the emergence, development, and criticism of Black Power concepts; Part II lists general materials used as background for the text.

I

BLACK POWER

Analavage, Robert. "A Victory in Defeat in Lowndes." *National Guardian,* Vol. 19, No. 7 (Nov. 19, 1966), p. 4.

Analavage, Robert. "Lowndes Party Girds for Future." *The Southern Patriot,* Vol. 24, No. 11 (Dec. 1966), p. 1.

Bailey, Gordon. "Big Rally in Watts Hears Carmichael." *The Militant,* Vol. 31, No. 44 (Dec. 5, 1966), p. 1.

Baldwin, James and Schulberg, Budd. "Dialog in Black and White." *Playboy,* Vol. 13, No. 12 (Dec. 1966), p. 133.

Barnes, Elizabeth. "Black Power." *Young Socialist,* Aug.-Sept., 1966, p. 12.

Bennett, Lerone, Jr. "Stokely Carmichael: Architect of Black Power." *Ebony,* Vol. XXI, No. 11 (Sept. 1966), p. 25.

Benson, Dr. George S. "Looking Ahead," *Column,* Searcy, Arkansas, Sept. 29, 1966.

Benson, Dr. George S. "Looking Ahead," *Column,* Searcy, Arkansas, Oct. 18, 1966.

Benson, John. "Interview with Stokely Carmichael." *The Militant,* May 23, 1966.

"Black Power" (editorial). *The New Republic,* Vol. 154, No. 25 (June 18, 1966), p. 5.

"Black Power." Flyer published by Constructive Action, Inc., La Jola, Calif., Summer 1966.

"Black Power and the White Radical." *19: A Radical Newspaper of the Committee for Independent Political Action,* Vol. 1, No. 4 (Oct. 21, 1966), p. 4.

"Black Power: The Widening Dialogue." *New South,* Vol. 21, No. 3 (Summer 1966), p. 65.

Bone, Richard. "A Black Man's Quarrel With the Christian God." *New York Times Book Review,* Sept. 11, 1966, p. 4.

115

Braden, Anne: "The SNCC Trends: Challenge to White America." *The Southern Patriot*, Vol. 24, No. 5 (May 1966), p. 1.

Carmichael, Stokely. Speech at Mt. Holyoke College, Nov. 16, 1966 (text printed in *Massachusetts Quarterly Review*, Dec. 1966).

Carmichael, Stokely. "Symposium." *Negro Digest*, Oct. 1966, p. 59.

Carmichael, Stokely. "What We Want." *The New York Review of Books*, Sept. 22, 1966, p. 5.

Cloward, Richard A. and Piven, Frances F. "Desegregated Housing." *The New Republic*, Vol. 155, No. 25 (Dec. 17, 1966), p. 17.

"Coming: Wide-Open Split Among Negro Leaders." *The National Observer*, Vol. 5, No. 41 (Oct. 10, 1966), p. 1.

Cook, Dr. Samuel D. "The Tragic Myth of Black Power." *New South*, Vol. 21, No. 3 (Summer 1966), p. 58.

Danzig, David. "In Defense of Black Power." *Commentary*, Vol. 41, No. 9 (Sept. 1966), p. 41.

Detwiler, Bruce. "A Time to Be Black." *The New Republic*, Vol. 155, No. 12 (Sept. 17, 1966), p. 19.

"Excerpts From Paper on Which the 'Black Power' Philosophy Is Based." *The New York Times*, Vol. CXV, No. 39,640 (Aug. 5, 1966), p. 10.

Fager, C. E. "White Reflections on Black Power." *The Christian Century*, Vol. LXXXIII, No. 32 (Aug. 10, 1966), p. 980.

Farmer, James. *Freedom — When?* New York, 1965.

Fiddick, Thomas C. "Black Power, Capitalism and Vietnam." *Liberation*, Vol. XI, No. 6 (Sept. 1966), p. 23.

Good, Paul. "A White Look at Black Power." *The Nation*, Vol. 203, No. 4 (Aug. 18, 1966), p. 112.

Hall, A.; Height, D.; Randolph, A. P.; Reynolds, H. R.; Rustin, B.; Wilkins, R. and Young, W. "Crisis and Commitment." Advertisement, *The New York Times*, Vol. CXVI, No. 39,710 (Oct. 14, 1966).

Hamilton, Charles V. "Mr. Charlie ... We'd Rather Do It Ourselves." Unpublished ms., Dept. of Political Science, Lincoln University, Pennsylvania.

"It Is Not Sufficient Merely to Condemn Black Power." Advertisement, *The New York Times*, Vol. CXV, No. 39,630 (July 26, 1966), p. 23.

Jehlen, Alen. "Black Power and Political Strategy." *new left notes*, Vol. 1, No. 42 (Nov. 11, 1966), p. 1.

King, Rev. Dr. Martin Luther, Jr. "Black Power." *The Progressive*, Vol. 30, No. 11 (Nov. 1966), p. 12.

Lawson, James M., Jr. "Black Power and the Mississippi March." *Fellowship*, Sept. 1966, p. 18.

National Broadcasting Co. *Meet the Press*, Aug. 21, 1966. Text printed by Merkle Press, Washington, D.C.

National Committee of Negro Churchmen. "Black Power." Advertisement, *The New York Times*, Vol. CXV, No. 39,635 (July 31, 1966).

"A Negro Congressman Talks About Black Power." *U. S. News and World Report*, Vol. LXI, No. 7 (Aug. 15, 1966), p. 37.

Nordin, K. "Interview with Stokely Carmichael." *The Christian Science Monitor*, Sept. 22, 1966, p. 10.

Phillips, John F. "Black Power." *The Scarlet and Black* (Grinnell College, Grinnell, Iowa), Sept. 9, 1966.

"A Power Player Sets the Goals." *Newsweek*, Vol. LXVIII, No. 8 (Aug. 22, 1966), p. 36.

Price, Wm. A. "SNCC Charts a Course — an Interview with Stokely Carmichael, Chairman, Student Nonviolent Coordinating Committee." *The National Guardian*, June 4, 1966.

Roberts, Gene. "Negro Nationalism a Black Power Key." *The New York Times*, Vol. CXV, No. 39,628 (July 24, 1966), p. 1.

Roberts, Gene. "The Story of SNCC — From 'Freedom High' to 'Black Power.'" *The New York Times Magazine*, Sept. 25, 1966, p. 27.

Rowan, Carl T. "Crisis in Civil Rights Leadership." *Ebony*, Vol. XXII, No. 1 (Nov. 1966), p. 27.

Rustin, Bayard. "Black Power and Coalition Politics." *Commentary*, Vol. 41, No. 9 (Sept. 1966), p. 35.

Sheppard, Barry. "Black Power Attacked by Old-Guard Leaders." *The Militant*, Vol. 30, No. 38 (Oct. 24, 1966), p. 1.

Sheppard, Barry. "Interview With CORE Leader." *The Militant*, Aug. 8, 1966, p. 5.

Sinclair, John. "Stokely in Detroit: Who's Afraid of Black Power?" *The Fifth Estate*, Vol. 1, No. 16 (Oct. 16-31), p. 1.

"SNCC-1966. Comments by Stokely Carmichael, Chairman Student Nonviolent Coordinating Committee." Published by SNCC, no place, no date.

Stone, I. F. "SNCC Does Not Wish To Become A New Version of the White Man's Burden." *I. F. Stone's Weekly*, June 6, 1966.

Stone, I. F. "Why They Cry Black Power." *I. F. Stone's Weekly*, Vol. XIV, No. 28 (Sept. 19, 1966), p. 1.

Wechsler, James A. "'Killers of the Dream.'" *The Progressive*, Vol. 30, No. 12 (December 1966), p. 12.

Weinraub, Bernard. "The Brilliancy of Black." *Esquire*, Vol. LXVII, No. 1 (Jan. 1967), p. 130.

Wilkins, Roy. "Separatism in 'Black Power' Seen by Wilkins." Letter to Editor, *The New York Times*, Vol. CXVI, No. 39,727 (Oct. 31, 1966), p. 34.

Wilkins, Roy. "Whither 'Black Power'?" *The Crisis*, Vol. 73, No. 7 (Aug.-Sept. 1966), p. 353.

Wilson, C. E. "Black Power and the Myth of Black Racism." *Liberation*, Vol. XI, No. 6 (Sept. 1966), p. 27.

X, Malcolm, with the assistance of Haley, Alex. *The Autobiography of Malcolm X*. New York, 1964.

II

GENERAL

Archer, Mrs. Elsie. *Let's Face It*. Philadelphia, 1959.

Bennett, Lerone, Jr. *Before the Mayflower*. Revised ed. Chicago, 1964.

Broderick, Francis L. and Meier, August. *Negro Protest Thought in the Twentieth Century*. Indianapolis, 1965.

Clark, Kenneth B. *Dark Ghetto*. 1st ed. New York, 1965.

Fischer, John. "Letter to a New Leftist, From a Tired Liberal." *Harper's*, Vol. 232, No. 1390 (Mar. 1966), p. 16.

Hadden, Jeffrey K. and Rymph, Raymond C. "The Marching Ministers." *Trans-ACTION*, Vol. 3, No. 5 (Sept.-Oct. 1966), p. 38.

"HEW Learns a Lesson." *Newsweek*, Vol. LXVI, No. 16 (Oct. 18, 1966), p. 98.

Jacobs, Paul and Landau, Saul. *The New Radicals*. New York, 1966.

Rustin, Bayard. "From Protest to Politics." Reprinted in Jacobs and Landau, *The New Radicals*, New York, 1966, p. 295.

"Say It Isn't So, Sargent Shriver." *The New York Times*, Vol. CXVI, No. 39 (Oct. 19, 1966), p. 35.

"Shriver Comes Across." *The New Republic*, Vol. 156, No. 1 (Jan. 7, 1966), p. 10.

Silberman, Charles E. *Crisis in Black and White*. New York, 1964.

Stampp, Kenneth. *The Peculiar Institution*. New York, 1956.

Voorhis, Jerry. *American Cooperatives: Where They Come From, What They Do, Where They Are Going*. New York, 1961.

Warren, Robert Penn. *Who Speaks for the Negro?* New York, 196?

Wechsler, James A. "Labor in Retreat: The AFL-CIO Tragedy." *The Progressive*, Vol. 31, No. 1 (Jan. 1966), p. 12.

Young, Whitney M., Jr. *To Be Equal*. 1st ed. New York, 1964.